# BUSHA BROWNE'S

*Indispensable
Compendium
of Traditional
Jamaican
Cookery*

*THE MILL PRESS*
*Kingston, Jamaica*

First published in 1993 by The Mill Press Limited

THE MILL AT CONSTANT SPRING
P.O. Box 167, Kingston 8
JAMAICA, WEST INDIES
Telephone: (809) 925-6886
Fax: (809) 931-1301

© 1993 The Mill Press Limited
*Part of the Jamaica Remembered Series*

National Library of Jamaica Cataloguing in Publication Data

Busha Browne's indispensable compendium
of traditional Jamaican cookery. – Rev. ed.
p. ; ill. ; c. – (The Jamaica remembered
series, ISSN 0799-0189 ; 2)

ISBN 976-8092-89-0 (pbk)

1. Cookery, Jamaican
I. Facey, Valerie    II. Series
641.5'97292-dc  20

Enquiries may be sent to The Mill Press
or directly to
Busha Browne's Company
P.O. Box 386, Newport East
Kingston
JAMAICA, WEST INDIES

Produced and published by the Mill Press Limited
Kingston, Jamaica

# Contents

# Introduction

## The Busha Browne Story

IN 1836, HOWE PETER BROWNE, 2nd Marquess of Sligo, returned to Westport, Ireland, taking with him fond memories of the spicy and exotic dishes he had been served during his governorship of Jamaica.

Known as "The Emancipator of the Slaves", the noble Marquess had earned himself a renowned place in Jamaican history for his two year term of office. His had been the unenviable task of supervising the first stage of Emancipation which was unpopular with the reactionary planters for whom the abolition of slavery assuredly meant financial ruin. In desperation many of these planters subsequently sold their vast estates to the local managers who were known as "BUSHAS".

Sligo himself was among the first to free his slaves on his Jamaican estates—Kelly's and Cocoa Walks—which he had inherited from his ancestors, the Kellys and Brownes of Ireland; Jamaican settlers from the late 1600s. The Brownes became wealthy and were numbered among the respected members of the plantocracy who were famous for their entertaining and the variety of food they served. In Jamaica their name has always been pronounced "BROWNEY".

A descendant of the family Sligo, Charles Adolphus Thorburn Browne—familiarly known as Charlie Browne—has spent most of his 75 years "cooking up a storm". He whiled away many hours of his boyhood days in the kitchen of his family home, Tryall Estate in Hanover, western Jamaica. Later, cooking became a hobby and he retrieved from his family archives recipes for authentic Jamaican sauces, jams, pickles and condiments made from the great variety of exotic Jamaican fruits and vegetables: all unique, spicy and delicious. Specially selected recipes from this treasure trove are now being prepared and bottled for Busha Browne's Company in Jamaica to be enjoyed today as much as they were over 200 years ago.

# About Jamaican Cookery

JAMAICAN COOKERY differs from that of the other West Indian Islands by reason of Jamaica's slightly different ethnic mix. The remnant of a pre-Columbian menu lingers on in the use of cassava and other indigenous provisions used by the original Arawak Indians. The short-lived Spanish supremacy remains with the commodities introduced by the Spaniards such as sugar cane, the banana, the orange and many other fruits and vegetables, as well as cattle, sheep, the pig, the chicken and the honeybee.

With the Spanish in 1494 came the Jews, and between them we now enjoy Escoveitched Fish, Solomon Gundy, Gizzadas and other ultra-palatable recipes. From 1655 the British taught us how to make custards and dumplings. Through the later East Indian, Middle Eastern and Chinese immigrants, additional influences such as rice and the legendary "curried goat" were added to the national cuisine.

The largest legacy of all has been the predominant African influence, principally in the use of the ackee, yams, dasheen, and other delectables such as Duckanoo or "Blue Drawers". These dishes are today valued for their taste and economy and have joined the ranks of the now popular Rastafarian trend in what, in Jamaica, is called *Ital* or *Soul Food*, while overseas it is termed *Roots Fare*, *Island Shack Food* or *Yard Style* eating.

West Indian food in general is spicy, but Jamaican food calls for a unique combination of "seasoning" for meats and savouries which includes lime juice, garlic and the incomparable, very hot but elusively flavourful Jamaican Scotch Bonnet Pepper. However, the secret ingredient in most Jamaican cookery is the indigenous pimento berry or "Allspice". It is the judicious addition of this mysterious, pungent spice that provides the exotic taste that highlights Jamaican cuisine in dishes as varied as soups and stews to fruit compotes and Jamaican Christmas Pudding.

By providing some of the finest gourmet products to the world, Busha Browne has become one of Jamaica's best ambassadors. The condiments and preserves complementing the time honoured dishes that are so dear to all Jamaicans can now become favourites worldwide.

**BUSHA BROWNE'S**
*Fine*
*JAMAICAN*
*Produce*

# About The Products

### Busha Browne's Pepper Jellies

The traditional spicy-sweet condiment based on the famous hot and flavourful Jamaican Scotch Bonnet Pepper.

*Original Pepper Jelly* is the perfect accompaniment for all meats, hot or cold, and excels when mixed with cream cheese for canapés or used as a spread or a dip. *Lime* is particularly good with fish while *Ginger* goes well with Chinese and Indian dishes.

Each of these exotic flavours complements a variety of foods including sandwiches and snacks. They also make a superb glaze for meats and vegetables.

### Busha Browne's Chutneys

Genuine Jamaican relishes that add the finishing touch to curries or stews and are superb with cold meats, poultry or game.

*Spicy Fruit*, a slightly firmer chutney, is excellent when added to recipes for interest or used in sandwiches. *Original Banana Chutney* is positively addictive. Try adding a teaspoonful to an icy cold mulligatawny soup—or a good dollop on vanilla ice cream.

### Busha Browne's Preserves

*Burned Orange Marmalade* is a distinctively different marmalade, darker and with a caramelized wild orange flavour. *Twice Boiled Guava Jelly* is equally unusual, being a rich and unctuous, characteristically flavourful spread.

Both preserves are redolent of the tropics and are delicious on toast or used in elegant desserts.

# Busha Browne's
## Pepper Jellies, Chutneys & Preserves

# Busha Browne's
## Sauces, Seasoning & Pepper Sherry

# Busha Browne's Sauces

Each of the collection of spicy sauces is superlative in its own way.

*Busha Browne's Original Spicy Planters Sauce* is the doyen of sauces which transforms casseroles and stews and enhances all meat, fowl and seafood dishes. An aged sauce of prestige, this authentic blend of mangoes, raisins, onions, tamarinds, tomatoes, peppers and spices is a trustworthy stalwart to be kept on hand at all times.

*Busha Browne's Spicy Tomato Love-Apple Sauce* is a distinguished tomato and basil-based blend, endowed with a spicy zip to liven pasta and seafood recipes or any other savoury dish. Excellent with scrambled eggs.

Not for the fainthearted, *Busha Browne's Pukka Hot Pepper Sauce* is the ultimate sauce for the devotee of wickedly hot food. Made from fragrant fresh Jamaican Scotch Bonnet peppers, this sauce has stamina and an outstanding flavour. No pepper fanatic should be without it.

*Busha Browne's Spicy Jerk Sauce* is the quintessential taste of Jamaica—a hot, exotic blend of herbs and spices. To be used in the preparation of meats, poultry or seafood prior to grilling on the barbecue. A small amount provides a subtle addition for soups and stews.

# Busha Browne's Jerk Seasoning

*Busha Browne's Jerk Seasoning* is the authentic hot spicy seasoning paste especially compounded for the "jerking" of meat or fish. Used prudently prior to barbecuing, this seasoning will provide the most pungent flavour and an absolutely irresistible aroma.

# Busha Browne's Pepper Sherry

For the discerning palate, *Busha Browne's Spicy & Hot Pepper Sherry* is the supreme embellishment to add a magical taste to soups or stews and savoury drinks such as Bullshots and Bloody Marys. It is also ideal in the preparation of stir fry dishes.

> N.B. All of Busha Browne's sauces, seasoning and sherry may be used individually or in a variety of mixtures to create the basis for many versatile marinades.

# *About The Cookbook*

BUSHA BROWNE'S *Indispensable Compendium of Traditional Jamaican Cookery* is Busha Browne's definitive cookbook which has been adapted for modern day cooking.

This edition is intended to be an introduction to Jamaican cookery as well as to generally make known the traditional spicy Jamaican sauces and condiments which are now conveniently available worldwide by means of the range of Busha Browne's authentic and highly acclaimed fine Jamaican produce.

Once familiar with Busha Browne's products, there are unlimited exciting ways of using them, as varied as the kaleidoscope of inventive cookery itself. In fact, once initiated, few cooks—amateur or professional—can resist the incomparable flavour and acclaim that invariably accompany the use of these genuine Jamaican condiments. Their manner of use is easily adjusted to accommodate any taste bud requirements, from the most timid to the reckless!

The recipes in this cookbook have been carefully compiled to retain their ethnic personality while making them easily understood by international aficionados. Both American Standard and Metric measurement have been used. A comprehensive glossary can be found at the back of the book to explain any unrecognizable items and give an idea of what may be substituted according to the country and culture involved. Only seasonings specific to certain individual dishes have been included in the recipes, as most of the primary herbs and spices already form an integral part of the various Busha Browne's products themselves.

Following is a guideline for the symbols used in this book to indicate the "hotness" of a recipe. Busha Browne's products themselves are identified by the symbol ❖. The amounts of these products used can be freely increased or decreased, according to personal requirements.

🌴

Mildly Hot
(for the fainthearted)

🌴 🌴

Moderately Hot
(for the more adventurous)

🌴 🌴 🌴

Wickedly Hot
(for the inveterate pepper fiend)

# Preambles

The codfish lays ten thousand eggs,
The homely hen lays one
The codfish never cackles
To tell you what she's done.
And so we scorn the codfish
While the humble hen we prize
Which only goes to show you
That it pays to advertise.

—*Anonymous*

# Alligator Pear Relish

Lady Nugent, wife of General George Nugent, Governor of Jamaica from 1802-5, refers to avocado as 'subaltern's butter' in her Journal. The impecunious junior officers of the British Army, stationed in Jamaica, would use this cheap fruit to spread on their bread instead of using butter, which was expensive and difficult to keep in the tropical Jamaican climate prior ro refrigeration.

🌴 🌴

| 1 | Ripe avocado | 1 |
|---|---|---|
| 1 tbsp | Lime or lemon juice | 15 ml |
| ¼ tsp | Salt | 1 ml |
| ⅛ tsp | Freshly ground black pepper | .5 ml |
| 1 tbsp | ❖ Busha Browne's Original Spicy Planters Sauce | 15 ml |
| Dash | ❖ Busha Browne's Pukka Hot Pepper Sauce | Dash |

Crush avocado lightly and immediateiy sprinkle with lime or lemon juice to prevent a change of colour. Add the salt, pepper, *Planters Sauce* and *Pukka Sauce*. Mix lightly with fork. Serve at once with breadfruit chips, pita bread triangles or crisp crackers or toast.
VARIATION: *The addition of a small amount of minced black olives or finely chopped smoked oysters or grated onion gives another dimension to this relish.*

# Avocado Canoes

🌴

| 1 | Small ripe avocado | 1 |
|---|---|---|
| 1 tsp | Lime or lemon juice | 5 ml |
| | Salt to taste | |
| | Freshly ground black pepper to taste | |
| 4 oz | Steamed miniature shrimp | 125 g |
| 1 tbsp | ❖ Busha Browne's Spicy Tomato Love-Apple Sauce | 15 ml |
| 1 tbsp | ❖ Busha Browne's Original Spicy Planters Sauce | 15 ml |

Halve avocado, and remove seed. Sprinkle each half with lime or lemon juice, and fill with half the cooked shrimp, which has been tossed with the *Spicy Tomato Sauce*. Serve on a plate garnished with lettuce leaves, with salt and pepper on the side. Eat with a teaspoon.
VARIATION: *Sprinkle the avocado halves with lime or lemon juice and serve filled with Planters Sauce. Remarkable!*

# Miniature Meat Quenelles

Makes about 175 bite-size quenelles. These can be made and shaped well ahead of party time.

🌴

| | | |
|---|---|---|
| 3 lb | Ground chuck or round steak | 1.5 kg |
| ½ cup | Grated carrots | 125 ml |
| ¼ cup | Soy sauce | 60 ml |
| ¼ cup | ❖ Busha Browne's Original Spicy Planters Sauce | 60 ml |
| ¼ cup | ❖ Busha Browne's Spicy Tomato Love-Apple Sauce | 60 ml |
| 2 tsp | ❖ Busha Browne's Spicy Jerk Seasoning (optional) | 10 ml |
| 2 | Eggs, lightly beaten | 2 |
| ¾ cup | Water | 180 ml |
| 2 | Cloves garlic, put through a press | 2 |
| 2 tsp | Ground ginger | 10 ml |
| | Salt and pepper to taste | |

In a large bowl, combine the two or (three) *Busha Browne's Sauces*, water, garlic and ginger and mix until blended. Add the ground meat, carrots and eggs, and blend lightly but thoroughly. Using a teaspoon, lift out spoonfuls of meat mixture, shaping lightly with dampened hands into round balls under 1 inch(2.4 cm) in diameter. At this stage, if making ahead of time, cover tightly with plastic wrap and refrigerate. When ready to cook the quenelles, put them in a single layer on a large baking sheet in a slow oven 300° F (150°C) and bake uncovered for about 15 minutes, turning once. Serve a few at a time on toothpicks, keeping the rest warm in a low oven. Serve with dip.

VARIATION: *Fish, veal or chicken may be used instead of beef to make these delicate little morsels.*

# Chutney & Love-Apple Dip

🌴 🌴

| | | |
|---|---|---|
| ¾ cup | ❖ Busha Browne's Original Banana Chutney | 180 ml |
| ¼ cup | ❖ Busha Browne's Spicy Tomato Love-Apple Sauce | 60 ml |
| Dash | ❖ Busha Browne's Pukka Hot Pepper Sauce | Dash |
| 2 cups | Sour cream | 500 ml |
| 2 tbsp | Best Indian curry powder | 30 ml |

In a glass bowl combine the *Banana Chutney*, the *Spicy Tomato Sauce* and the *Pukka Sauce*. In a separate bowl mix the curry powder with the sour cream. Combine the two mixtures together to make a superb dip for crudités, Miniature Meat Quenelles, etc.

# Smoked Marlin in Aspic

Smoked Blue Marlin is Jamaica's answer to Smoked Salmon. Tag and Release tournaments are held each year specially aimed at capturing these big game fish. Marlin caught by local fishermen are smoked and served as an hors d'oeuvre, in salad or other dishes.

🌴

| | | |
|---|---|---|
| 4 tbsp | Gelatin, softened in 1 cup water | 60 ml |
| 3 cups | Concentrated chicken stock | 750 ml |
| ½ cup | Lime or lemon juice | 125 ml |
| ¼ cup | ❖ Busha Browne's Spicy & Hot Pepper Sherry | 60 ml |
| 1 cup | Diced red and green sweet peppers | 250 ml |
| 1 cup | Diced celery stalks | 250 ml |
| 3 cups | Flaked smoked marlin | 750 ml |
| | Extra virgin olive oil to brush mould. | |

Sprinkle gelatin on cold water to dissolve. Add boiling hot chicken stock to gelatin and stir until completely dissolved. Add lime juice and *Pepper Sherry*. Refrigerate and allow to partially set: add diced sweet pepper and celery. Fold in flaked smoked marlin. Put into mould which has been brushed with olive oil and allow to set firmly. Transfer from mould onto platter, garnish and serve immediately.

# Tryall Fish Paté

Tryall Estate, an elegant hotel and villa resort with an internationally famous golf course, was one of the family homes of the Jamaican Browne family.

🌴

| | | |
|---|---|---|
| 2 cups | Cooked white fish fillets, flaked fine | 500 ml |
| 2 | Cloves garlic, crushed | 2 |
| 2 tbsp | Grated onion | 30 ml |
| 1 tbsp | ❖ Busha Browne's Spicy & Hot Pepper Sherry | 15 ml |
| 1 tbsp | ❖ Busha Browne's Original Spicy Planters Sauce | 15 ml |
| ¼ tsp | Salt | 1 ml |
| 2 tbsp | Butter | 30 ml |

Skin fish, then combine with garlic, onion and salt in a bowl or blender. Add *Pepper Sherry* and *Planters Sauce*, varying amount according to taste and texture. Mixture should be the consistency of thick paste. Melt butter, then cool and add to fish mixture. Put in covered bowl and chill. Serve with crackers, triangles of pita bread or chunks of French bread. TIP: *Delicious made with smoked blue marlin.*

# Stamp & Go
## (Saltfish fritters)

Salted codfish fritters are prepared throughout the Caribbean.
The Jamaican version is known as 'Stamp & Go', allegedly
derived from the order given by officers on 18th century
sailing ships in the British Royal Navy when something had
to be done in a hurry.

🌴

| | | |
|---|---|---|
| ½ lb | Dried, salted codfish | 225 g |
| 1 tsp | ❖ Busha Browne's Spicy & Hot Pepper Sherry | 5 ml |
| 1 cup | All purpose flour (4 ozs) | 250 ml |
| 1 tsp | Baking powder | 5 ml |
| ¼ tsp | Salt | 1 ml |
| 1 | Egg, lightly beaten | 1 |
| ¾ cup | Milk | 180 ml |
| 1 tbsp | Butter, melted | 15 ml |
| 1 | Onion, finely chopped | 1 |
| ½ tsp | ❖ Busha Browne's Pukka Hot Pepper Sauce | 2 ml |
| 1 tbsp | ❖ Busha Browne's Original Spicy Planters Sauce | 15 ml |
| | Vegetable oil for deep frying. | |

Soak codfish in water to tenderize and remove salt. Drain, rinse and place
in a saucepan of cold water to cover; bring to the boil. Simmer until
tender. Drain fish, remove bones and skin, and shred finely.

Sift the flour, baking powder and salt together. Combine the egg, milk,
butter and *Pepper Sherry* and stir into the dry ingredients. Add the fish,
onion, the *Pukka Sauce* and the *Planters Sauce* and mix well. Drop by the
tablespoonful into hot oil 375° F (190° C) on a frying thermometer and
fry until golden brown.

Mixture should be runny enough so that the fritters spread to form thin
lacy patterns, which cook quickly to crispness. Drain on paper towels and
serve hot with a dip of *Busha Browne's Spicy Tomato Love-Apple Sauce* or
Spicy Cocktail Dip (see below). Makes about 24 crisp, lacy fritters.

# Busha Browne's Spicy Cocktail Dip
🌴 🌴

Mix ¼ cup each *Busha Browne's Original Spicy Planters Sauce* and *Busha
Browne's Spicy Tomato Love-apple Sauce* with a dash of *Busha Browne's
Spicy and Hot Pepper Sherry* to taste. Serve with Stamp & Go as a dip.
VARIATION: Add 1 cup (250 ml) sour cream, plain unsweetened yogurt or
*Busha Browne's Jiffy Mayonnaise (page 81)*.

# Jamaican Beef Patties

Best loved Jamaican snack, patties are now available in many major North American and British cities, taken there by emigrants from Jamaica.

🌴 🌴 🌴

| | Busha Browne's Savoury Pastry (doubled - page 79) | |
|---|---|---|
| | *adding* | |
| 1 tbsp | Curry powder | 15 ml |
| | FILLING | |
| 2 | Onions, finely diced | 2 |
| 3 | Stalks escallion, finely diced | 3 |
| 2 lb | Finely minced beef | 1 kg |
| ⅓ cup | Best quality vegetable oil | 80 ml |
| 2 cups | Dried breadcrumbs | 500 ml |
| 1 tsp | Dried thyme | 5 ml |
| 2 tbsp | ❖ Busha Browne's Original Spicy Planters Sauce | 30 ml |
| ½ tsp | ❖ Busha Browne's Pukka Hot Pepper Sauce | 2 ml |
| 1 tsp | Salt | 5 ml |
| ¼ tsp | Black pepper | 1 ml |
| 1 cup | Water (approximately) | 250 ml |

Lightly mix the finely ground beef with the diced onions and escallion. Heat the oil, and brown the meat mixture, then add the breadcrumbs, thyme and *Busha Browne's Sauces*, salt and pepper. Add a little water, cover and simmer for 30 minutes. The filling should come together but not be too dry nor too runny. Allow to cool.

Roll out pastry and cut 4 in (10 cm) circles. Put a spoonful of filling on each circle, then fold over and crimp edges. Bake on an ungreased cookie sheet in oven preheated to 400° F (200° C) for 30 to 35 minutes or until the pastry is golden brown. Makes about 24 cocktail patties.

## Busha Browne's Plantain Delight

🌴

| | | |
|---|---|---|
| 1 | Extra ripe plantain | 1 |
| 10 | Rashers bacon | 10 |
| 2 tbsp | ❖ Busha Browne's Original Pepper Jelly | 30 ml |

Slice ripe plantain into ten chunks. Wrap each chunk in a strip of bacon, securing with a toothpick. Bake in medium oven about 30 minutes or until plantain and bacon are cooked, brushing several times with melted *Pepper Jelly. Plump pre-soaked prunes may be substituted for the ripe plantain.*

# Villa de la Vega Quiche Squares

An elegant party dish reminiscent of the red brick and flagstone patterns of Spanish Town, Jamaica's capital for more than 300 years. Founded by the Spanish in 1534, it was originally named Villa de la Vega 'The Town on the Plain'.

🌴 🌴

| | Busha Browne's Savoury Pastry (page 79) | |
|---|---|---|
| 2 tbsp | All purpose flour | 30 ml |
| ¾ cup | Finely diced baked or boiled ham (6 ozs) | 180 ml |
| 1 cup | Grated Cheddar Cheese (8 ozs) | 250 ml |
| 2 | Whole eggs | 2 |
| 2 | Egg yolks | 2 |
| 1 cup | Milk | 250 ml |
| 1 cup | Evaporated milk | 250 ml |
| 1 tsp | ❖ Busha Browne's Spicy & Hot Pepper Sherry | 5 ml |
| 2 tbsp | ❖ Busha Browne's Original Spicy Planters Sauce | 30 ml |
| ½ tsp | ❖ Busha Browne's Pukka Hot Pepper Sauce | 2 ml |
| ½ tsp | Dried mustard | 2 ml |
| ½ tsp | Salt | 2 ml |
| ⅛ tsp | Pepper | .5 ml |
| 1 tsp | Freshly grated nutmeg | 5 ml |
| | Red sweet pepper | |
| | Black olives | |

Line a rectangular jellyroll pan with pastry, making the edge about ¾ in. (2 cm) high. Flour bottom of pastry in the pan. Arrange the diced ham in a layer and cover with the grated cheese.

Beat eggs and yolks with whisk, then add milk, cream, *Busha Browne's Sauces*, and seasoning. Pour mixture into pastry lined pan. Bake in oven preheated to 350° F(180° C) for 45 to 50 minutes or until filling is set and crust is lightly browned. Transfer carefully on to an attractive serving dish, garnish and serve hot, cut in 1½ in. (4 cms) squares. Decorate alternate squares with slivers of sautéed red sweet pepper and sliced black olives to create a checkerboard effect.

*Jellyroll pan: 10" x 15" x 1" deep or 25 cm x 38 cm x 2.5 cm deep.*

TO MAKE AHEAD: Line the pan with pastry, add the ham and cheese layers, cover with clear plastic wrap and store in refrigerator. Prepare the egg mixture, cover and refrigerate. About an hour before serving, pour egg mixture over ham and cheese and bake in oven preheated to 350°F (180°C). Makes approximately 48 squares.

TIP: *This recipe produces a better result if it is baked on the bottom rack of the preheated oven as the pastry bakes more crisply.*

# *Busha Browne's Variations on Cheese*
## *Baked Brie with Banana Chutney*

|  | *Busha Browne's Savoury Pastry (page 79) divided in two* |  |
|---|---|---|
| 2 lb | *Brie Cheese (22 oz)* | 1 kg |
| 1 cup | ❖ *Busha Browne's Original Banana Chutney* | 250 ml |

Line a 9 inch (23 cm) pie dish with half the pastry. Place a large wheel of brie cheese in the centre of the pie crust. Work crust up around sides of brie. Roll out second half of pastry, and cut into strips. Cover the top of the brie with *Banana Chutney*. Take strips of dough and weave a lattice across the top of the brie wheel pinching the strips to the sides. Place on rack in centre of hot oven, preheated to 425° F (200°C) and bake for 12-15 minutes or until crust is golden brown.

## *Busha Browne's Cheese Log*

*A block of Goat Cheese*
❖ *Busha Browne's Original Spicy Planters Sauce*

Place a block of goat or feta cheese on an oval plate, and smother with *Planters Sauce*. Serve with thin crisp crackers or pita bread, split and buttered, cut into triangles and toasted.

## *Jerk Cheese*

| 2 lb | *Best quality Cheddar Cheese (22 oz)* | 1 kg |
|---|---|---|
| ½ cup | ❖ *Busha Browne's Spicy Jerk Sauce* | 125 ml |

Freeze cheese overnight. Crumble while still frozen and combine with the *Spicy Jerk Sauce*. Compress into any moulded shape and serve.

## *Cheese 'N' Chutney*

Mix together cream cheese or feta cheese and *Busha Browne's Spicy Fruit Chutney* or *Busha Browne's Original Banana Chutney*. Serve with crackers, or crisp toast triangles. Garnish with a little of the chutney.

# Soups
# &
# Savouries
*(hot or cold—lusty or delicate)*

Beautiful soup, so rich and green,
Waiting in a Hot Tureen.
Who for such dainties would not stoop
Soup of the evening, beautiful soup.

*–Lewis Carroll*

# Busha Browne's Hearty Red Pea Soup

🌴 🌴

| | | |
|---|---|---|
| 2 cups | Red peas (red kidney beans) | 500 ml |
| 2 qt | Cold water | 2 l |
| 1½ cups | Fresh coconut milk (optional - see below) | 375 ml |
| 1 lb | Soup meat (shin is best) | 500 g |
| 4 | Rashers bacon, or a salted pig's tail (optional) | 4 |
| 1 tsp | ❖ Busha Browne's Pukka Hot Pepper Sauce | 5 ml |
| 1 | Coco (or 1 Irish potato) - sliced | 1 |
| 1 | Chopped onion | 1 |
| 1 | Sprig fresh thyme | 1 |
| 1 tbsp | ❖ Busha Browne's Original Spicy Planters Sauce | 15 ml |
| 1 tbsp | ❖ Busha Browne's Spicy Tomato Love-Apple Sauce | 15 ml |
| | Salt and pepper to taste | |
| ¼ cup | ❖ Busha Browne's Spicy & Hot Pepper Sherry | 60 ml |

Put peas to soak overnight. The following morning, drain the peas and discard water in which they were soaked. Put the 2 qt (2 l) of water and the coconut milk into a large saucepan. Add the meats and peas and the *Pukka Sauce*. Boil until peas are almost tender. Add coco (or potato) and seasonings, including *Planters Sauce* and *Spicy Tomato Sauce*. When peas and coco are cooked, remove the meats. Blend the liquid, the peas and the coco together, strain out the pea skins and discard; or put through a colander and rub out. In either case discard the skins. A few whole peas may be retained to serve with the soup if desired. Add *Pepper Sherry*.

Pass the bottle of *Pepper Sherry* for those who enjoy a more spicy dish. This soup is usually served with small, elongated flour dumplings known in Jamaica as "spinners" (page 78).

TIP: *Any left over soup may be frozen and reheated but may require additional liquid as it thickens on refrigeration.*

TIP: *Add 1 in (2.5 cm) bruised fresh ginger root or a teaspoonful of ground ginger to this soup to aid the digestion.*

## Coconut Milk

Coconut milk is made from a fresh dry coconut and is not sweetened. Use a hammer to break the hard shell and remove the pieces of firm white 'meat' with a sharp knife. (It is not necessary to remove the brown skin from the white meat.) Grate the 'meat' on a hand grater or in a food processor. Add 1 pint (500 ml) of hot water, press through a sieve or a brown calico bag. Discard the 'trash' and keep 'milk' in the refrigerator in a tightly capped bottle until required, but not longer than two days. Coconut milk may also be frozen. A medium sized coconut will yield approximately 2 cups (500 ml) of coconut milk.

# Traditional Jamaican
# Pepper Pot Soup

In her journal for 1802, Lady Nugent tells of a dinner of which she partook at Golden Grove in St Thomas and quotes the menu, and 'the receipt' for Black Crab Pepperpot:

"… A capon stewed down, a large piece of beef and another of ham, also stewed to a jelly; then six dozen of land crabs, picked fine, with their eggs and fat, onions, peppers, ochra, sweet herbs, and other vegetables of the country, cut small; and this well stewed, makes black crab pepperpot…"

🌴 🌴 🌴

| | | |
|---|---|---|
| 1 lb | Soup meat - beef or chicken | 500 g |
| 2 | Rashers bacon or a salted pig's tail (optional) | 2 |
| 2 lb | Callaloo, chopped coarsely | 1 kg |
| 1 lb | Indian kale, chopped | 500 g |
| 1½ cups | Fresh coconut milk (optional) | 375 ml |
| 2 qt | Cold water | 1 l |
| 1 dozen | Okras, sliced | 12 |
| 1 tsp | Oil | 1 |
| 1 | Chopped onion | 1 |
| 1 | Coco (or 1 Irish potato) diced coarsely | 1 |
| | Salt and pepper to taste | |
| 1 tbsp | ❖ Busha Browne's Original Spicy Planters Sauce | 15 ml |
| 1 tbsp | ❖ Busha Browne's Spicy Tomato Love-Apple Sauce | 15 ml |
| 2 tsp | ❖ Busha Browne's Pukka Hot Pepper Sauce | 10 ml |
| 6 | Black crabs | 6 |
| | or | |
| ½ lb | Precooked miniature shrimp | 250 g |
| | Spinners or dumplings (optional - page 78) | |

Mix coconut milk with water in a large pot. Add meats, callaloo, kale and black crabs tied in a cheesecloth bag. Cook until meats are tender. Remove black crabs and pick out the meat from the shells, particularly from the claws, including any roe: reserve and refrigerate.

Sauté sliced okra in oil, then add to boiling soup mixture with coco, onion, *Busha Browne's Sauces* and seasonings. Simmer until soup is thickened. If desired, purée or blend the soup. Add small round flour spinners or dumplings, and at last moment, return the crabmeat (or add precooked shrimp) and reheat. Adjust seasoning. Serve piping hot, in soup bowls with a slice of avocado pear, offering *Pepper Sherry*. Serves 8.
TIP: *This classic soup is improved by cooking over two days, allowing it to remain in the refrigerator to 'cogitate' between cookings.*

# Busha's Calabaza Pumpkin Soup

This recipe is typical of the one-pot meal that is so popular in Jamaica. Bunches of sliced vegetables tied together with banana trash were traditionally known as 'leggins'. This word is most likely a corruption of the French word 'légumes' and is a reminder of the small group of French immigrants who took refuge in Jamaica after the French Revolution of 1789.

🌴 🌴

| | | |
|---|---|---|
| 1 lb | Beef, preferably shin with marrow in bone | 500 g |
| 2 qt | Cold water | 2 l |
| 1 | Onion chopped coarsely | 1 |
| 2 - 3 | Stalks escallion, chopped | 2 - 3 |
| 1 tsp | Salt | 5 ml |
| 1 tsp | ❖ Busha Browne's Pukka Hot Pepper Sauce | 5 ml |
| | Bouquet garni made up of — | |
| | Bay leaf | |
| | French thyme, 2 leaves | |
| | Garlic clove, bruised, skin removed | |
| | Jamaican thyme, 2 sprigs | |
| | Pimento berries, (8) | |
| 2 lb | Dry Calabaza pumpkin, peeled, cut into chunks | 1 kg |
| 2 | Carrots, pared and cut in chunks | 2 |
| 1 | Celery stalk, chopped | 1 |
| 1 | Cho-cho, peeled and cut in chunks | 1 |
| 1 lb | Breadfruit or coco, peeled and chunked | 500 g |
| 1 tbsp | ❖ Busha Browne's Original Spicy Planters Sauce | 5 ml |
| | ❖ Busha Browne's Spicy & Hot Pepper Sherry | |
| | Dumplings or spinners or a mixture of both (page 78) | |
| | Nutmeg, freshly grated | |

Put the soup meat, onion, escallion, salt and bones into cold water in a large saucepan. Add *Pukka Sauce* and make up bouquet garni, either by tying all the herbs together in a calico/muslin bag or by threading them on to a toothpick, so that you can retrieve them before serving. Boil until meat is tender. Add the next five ingredients. Bring soup to the boil, then simmer for about an hour or until vegetables are thoroughly cooked. Add *Busha Browne's Sauces*. Correct seasoning if required.

If desired, remove the meat, reserve, and blend all other ingredients until smooth, or rub through a fine colander. A blender is better than a food processor as there is a fair amount of liquid. Add dumplings and cook until they rise to the surface. Cut meat into small bits and return to the soup with the marrow bones if available. Ladle soup into bowls, making sure that each serving contains bits of meat and several dumplings.

Garnish with freshly grated nutmeg and serve piping hot. Serves 6 - 8.

# Breadfruit Vichyssoise Captain Bligh

The breadfruit is much prized in Jamaica. After his initial attempt to introduce this tree to the island failed, Captain William Bligh, of the *Bounty* mutiny fame, triumphantly arrived at Port Royal in 1793 with 347 plants aboard *HMS Providence*. These were planted in several of the botanical gardens, as well as other designated areas of Jamaica and today provide a most beautiful tree and an important food crop islandwide.

🌴 🌴

| | | |
|---|---|---|
| 2 tbsp | Butter | 30 ml |
| 2 | Large onions, finely minced | 2 |
| 2 | Garlic cloves put through press | 2 |
| 1½ cups | Peeled breadfruit, diced | 375 ml |
| 2 cups | Concentrated chicken stock | 500 ml |
| ½ tsp | ❖ Busha Browne's Pukka Hot Pepper Sauce | 2 ml |
| 1 tbsp | ❖ Busha Browne's Original Spicy Planters Sauce | 15 ml |
| ½ tsp | Salt | 2 ml |
| ⅛ tsp | Freshly grated nutmeg | .5 ml |
| 1 cup | Light cream or plain unsweetened yogurt | 250 ml |
| 2 tbsp | Finely chopped green escallion tops | 30 ml |

Melt butter in skillet, sauté onions and garlic until transparent. Add the uncooked breadfruit, stock, *Busha Browne's sauces* and seasonings. Simmer covered until breadfruit is tender. Cool. Put through colander or blend. Add the cream or the yogurt and stir until smooth. Correct seasoning. Chill thoroughly and serve in chilled bowls, garnished with chopped green escallion tops. Serves 4.
VARIATION: *Irish potatoes or yellow yam may be used instead of breadfruit.*

# Jellied Consommé Supreme

🌴

| | | |
|---|---|---|
| 1½ cups | Best quality consommé | 375 ml |
| 1 tbsp | ❖ Busha Browne's Spicy & Hot Pepper Sherry | 15 ml |
| 1 tsp | Unflavoured gelatine | 5 ml |
| ½ cup | Cold water | 125 ml |

In a saucepan heat the consommé to point of boiling. Sprinkle gelatine over cold water to dissolve and add to hot consommé stirring until the gelatine is melted and thoroughly dispersed. Cool slightly then add the *Pepper Sherry*. Pour into glass bowl and refrigerate overnight to set. Spoon the set consommé into prechilled bowls and garnish with a wedge of lime and a few freshly ground paw paw seeds or black pepper. Serves 2.

# Avocado & Paw Paw Gazpacho

Said of this recipe: "Pukka does not burn the mouth. It warms the heart and soul."

🌴 🌴 🌴

| | | |
|---|---|---|
| 1 cup | Firm, ripe paw paw, finely chopped | 250 ml |
| 1 cup | Firm, ripe avocado, finely chopped | 250 ml |
| ⅓ cup | Sweet green pepper, finely chopped | 80 ml |
| ⅔ cup | Firm, ripe tomatoes | 160 ml |
| ¼ cup | Sweet onion, finely chopped | 60 ml |
| 3 cups | Best quality tomato juice | 750 ml |
| 3 cups | Fresh, unsweetened pineapple juice | 750 ml |
| 1 tsp | Fresh lime or lemon juice | 5 ml |
| 1 tsp | ❖ Busha Browne's Pukka Hot Pepper Sauce | 5 ml |
| | Salt and freshly ground black pepper to taste | |

Combine all the finely chopped ingredients in a glass bowl and chill for several hours. Serve icy cold in prechilled earthenware bowls garnished with a few freshly ground paw paw seeds, a sprig of cilantro or young celery tops. Serves 6.

# Treasure Beach Conch Soup

🌴 🌴 🌴

| | | |
|---|---|---|
| 1½ lb | Conch meat | 750 g |
| 1 tsp | Lime or lemon juice | 5 ml |
| 2 qts | Cold water | 2 l |
| 1 cup | Coconut milk (optional - page 20) | 250 ml |
| 1 tsp | ❖ Busha Browne Pukka Hot Pepper Sauce | 5 ml |
| ½ cup | Cho-cho, diced | 125 ml |
| ½ cup | Carrots, diced | 125 ml |
| ½ cup | Firm ripe tomatoes | 125 ml |
| 1½ cups | Irish potatoes, diced raw | 750 ml |
| | Salt and ground black pepper to taste | |
| | Red sweet pepper, chopped | |

Rub cleaned conch meat with lime juice and cut into small cubes. Boil in water with *Pukka Sauce* and coconut milk for approximately two hours. Add vegetables, salt and pepper and simmer until vegetables are tender. Serve in coconut shell bowls garnished with red sweet pepper.
VARIATION: *May also be made with crab, lobster or scallops.*
TIP: *May be served either piping hot or very cold. Garnish accordingly.*

# Busha Browne's Special Mulligatawny

The word "Mulligatawny" comes from two East Indian (Tamil)
words: molagu (pepper) and tanni (water). This soup has
evolved gracefully from its humble beginnings to become an
unusual treat to be enjoyed in the finest eating places.

🌴 🌴 🌴

| | | |
|---|---|---|
| 4 cups | Concentrated chicken or beef stock | 1 l |
| 4 tbsp | Unsalted butter | 60 ml |
| ½ cup | Onion, diced | 125 ml |
| | Clove of garlic, finely chopped | |
| 1½ tsp | Best Indian curry powder | 7 ml |
| | A pinch of ground cloves | |
| 1 tsp | ❖ Busha Browne's Pukka Hot Pepper Sauce | 5 ml |
| 2 tsp | ❖ Busha Browne's Original Spicy Planters Sauce | 10 ml |
| ½ cup | Purée of mammee apple with ½ tsp (2 ml) lime juice | 125 ml |
| | or | |
| ½ cup | Purée of dried tart apricots | 125 ml |
| 1 tbsp | Arrowroot | 15 ml |
| 1 cup | Pre-cooked gungo peas or lentils | 250 ml |
| | Salt and pepper to taste | |
| 1 cup | Plain unsweetened yogurt, icy cold | 250 ml |
| | ❖ Busha Browne's Original Banana Chutney | |

Reserve ½ cup (125 ml) of cold stock before heating. In a deep skillet,
sauté onion and garlic in the butter. Add in order, while stirring, curry
powder, cloves, *Busha Browne's Sauces*, the purée of mammee apple (or
apricots) and the gungo peas (or lentils). Gradually stir in hot meat stock
and simmer for 20 minutes. Mix arrowroot with reserved cold stock. Add
slowly to hot mixture, and continue to cook over low heat, stirring
continuously, until thickened. Correct seasoning. Chill overnight. Just
before serving, add the icy cold plain unsweetened yogurt and garnish
each bowl with a generous dollop of *Banana Chutney*. Serves 6.
VARIATION: *Mulligatawny may also be used hot as an accompaniment to a rice
meal and is served with side dishes of grated fresh coconut, chopped hard boiled
eggs, sliced banana, chopped peanuts, raisins, chopped sweet onions and Spicy
Fruit Chutney. (See "Sambals" - page 65)*

## Grated Coconut

Freshly grated coconut is made from a fresh dried coconut and is not
sweetened. Use a hammer to break the hard shell. With a sharp knife
remove the 'meat' which must then be peeled if pure white coconut is
desired. Grate the meat on a hand grater or in a food processor. Keep
refrigerated in a plastic bag until required. Use within two days.

# Busha Browne's Spicy Cheese Toast

🌴 🌴

| | | |
|---|---|---|
| 4 - 6 | Slices of brown bread | 4 - 6 |
| ½ cup | Grated Cheddar Cheese | 125 ml |
| 2 tsp | ❖ Busha Browne's Spicy Tomato Love-Apple Sauce | 10 ml |
| ½ tsp | ❖ Busha Browne's Original Spicy Planters Sauce | 2 ml |
| 2 tsp | Milk or cream | 10 ml |
| 1 tbsp | Soft butter | 15 ml |

Combine cheese, *Spicy Tomato Sauce*, *Planters Sauce* and milk, mixing to a smooth paste. Spread bread slices first with butter then with cheese paste. Grill until bubbling and brown. Serves 2 - 3.

# Planter's Savoury Pasta Quiche

🌴

| | | |
|---|---|---|
| 6 oz | Macaroni | 180 g |
| ½ lb | Sharp Cheddar Cheese | 250 g |
| 1 | Medium onion | 1 |
| 2 slices | Cooked ham, chopped (optional) | 2 slices |
| ½ cup | Snow peas (optional) | 125 ml |
| 2 | Whole eggs | 2 |
| 1 cup | Milk | 250 ml |
| ½ tsp | Dry mustard | 2 ml |
| 1 tbsp | ❖ Busha Browne's Original Spicy Planters Sauce | 15 ml |
| ¼ tsp | Salt | 1 ml |
| 1 | Tomato, sliced (optional) | 1 |

Cook macaroni until al dente and drain. Do not overcook. Grate cheese, and chop onion finely. In mixing bowl, whip eggs until frothy, then add milk, mustard, salt and *Planters Sauce*. Butter a 1½ pint (750 ml) oven-proof casserole and assemble ingredients by layering. Use half the macaroni first in the bottom of the casserole, then sprinkle with half the chopped onion, half the ham, half the snow peas and half the grated cheese. Make a second layer ending with grated cheese. Stir the milk and egg mixture, and pour over the macaroni mixture. Decorate if desired with sliced tomato and additional snow peas. Place casserole in a roasting pan of hot water to a depth of 1 inch (2.5 cm) and bake in centre of preheated 350° F (180° C) oven for about 45 minutes, or until knife inserted halfway between edge and centre comes out clean. Serve hot or cold. Serves 4.

# Saltfish & Callaloo Quiche

🌴 🌴

| | | |
|---|---|---|
| 1 recipe | Busha Browne's Savoury Pastry (page 79) | 1 |
| ¼ lb | Dried salted cod fish | 125 g |
| 1 lb | Callaloo, steamed and chopped | 500 g |
| 2 cups | Milk | 500 ml |
| 3 | Whole eggs | 3 |
| ¼ tsp | Salt | 1 ml |
| ½ tsp | White pepper | 2 ml |
| ½ tsp | ❖ Busha Browne's Pukka Hot Pepper Sauce | 5 ml |
| 1 tsp | ❖ Busha Browne's Original Spicy Planters Sauce | 5 ml |
| 1 tsp | Chopped chives or escallions | 5 ml |

Boil and flake cod fish. Mix with callaloo and place in a pie dish lined with pastry. Beat eggs; add milk and seasonings, including *Pukka Sauce* and *Planters Sauce*. Pour over fish and callaloo mixture. Sprinkle the chopped chives or escallions on top. Bake in 350° F (180° C) oven for about 45 minutes, or until a knife inserted halfway between edge and centre of the quiche comes out clean. Serves 4.

# Mushroom & Sweet Pepper Frittata

🌴

| | | |
|---|---|---|
| 4 | Large brown eggs | 4 |
| 1 tbsp | ❖ Busha Browne's Original Spicy Planter's Sauce | 15 ml |
| ½ tsp | Salt | 2 ml |
| 2 cups | Sliced mushrooms | 500 ml |
| 1½ cups | Mixed red, yellow & green sweet peppers, julienne | 375 ml |
| ¼ cup | Chopped escallion including green tops | 60 ml |
| 1 tbsp | Extra virgin olive oil | 15 ml |
| 2 tbsp | ❖ Busha Browne's Spicy Tomato Love-Apple Sauce | 30 ml |

Preheat oven to 300° F (150°C). Place eggs, *Planters Sauce* and salt in bowl and beat well. Brush heavy, ovenproof skillet with olive oil, and when hot, add mushrooms and sauté for 3 to 4 minutes. Add sweet peppers, onion, garlic and escallion. Sauté for 2 to 3 minutes longer.

Remove skillet from heat and add egg mixture stirring gently. Place skillet in oven for about 5 minutes to set eggs. Cut into attractive portions and serve, garnished with *Spicy Tomato Sauce*. Serves 4.

VARIATION: *Sprinkle ¼ cup (60 ml) grated cheddar cheese over the top for the last 2 minutes in the oven.*

# Pukka Cheese Soufflé

🌴 🌴

| | Busha Browne's Classic Béchamel Sauce (page 80) | |
|---|---|---|
| ½ tsp | Paprika | 1 ml |
| ½ tsp | ❖ Busha Browne's Pukka Hot Pepper Sauce | 2 ml |
| 1 tsp | ❖ Busha Browne's Original Spicy Planters Sauce | 5 ml |
| ½ lb | Sharp Cheddar Cheese, grated | 250 g |
| 8 | Eggs, separated and beaten separately | 8 |

Make Busha Browne's Classic Béchamel Sauce, adding paprika and the Busha Browne's Sauces, mixing well. Add the grated cheese, stirring until it melts. Remove from heat. Beat the egg yolks until they are light in colour, and pour them gradually into the cheese sauce. With clean beaters, beat the egg whites ina separate bowl until they are stiff, but not dry. Fold the cheese sauce gradually into the egg whites. Pour into a souffle dish,which has been brushed with butter and dusted with flour, and bake for 10 minutes in a hot oven 475°F (240°C), then reduce heat to 400°F (200°C) and bake 25 minutes longer. Serves 6.
VARIATION: *Cheese may be reduced by half and a cup of chopped steamed callaloo or boiled ackees added.*

# Busha Browne's Planter's Rarebit

🌴

| 1 tbsp | Butter | 15 ml |
|---|---|---|
| 1 tbsp | All purpose flour | 15 ml |
| 3 tbsp | Milk | 40 ml |
| 2 tbsp | Red Stripe Beer | 30 ml |
| 1 tsp | Prepared mustard | 5 ml |
| 1 tsp | ❖ Busha Browne's Original Spicy Planters Sauce | 5 ml |
| 6 ozs | Grated Cheddar Cheese | 180 g |
| | Salt and pepper to taste | |
| 4 | Slices buttered toast, cut in two | 4 |

Heat the butter in a saucepan, and stir in the flour. Cook for several minutes, stirring well. Add the milk slowly and stir continually over low heat until the mixture thickens; then add the beer, the mustard, *Planters Sauce*, the cheese and the salt and pepper. Cook only until the cheese melts. Do not overcook or the mixture will become oily. Spread on the slices of buttered toast and put under a hot grill until golden brown. Serve at once. Serves 2. *Banana* or *Spicy Fruit Chutney* go well with rarebit.
VARIATION: *Top each slice of toast with slices of tomato, then warm under the grill and top with the cheese mixture.*

# Salads
## &
# Vegetable Bounty
### (drest & undrest)

Four persons are wanted
To make a good salad—
A Spendthrift for oil,
A Miser for vinegar,
A Counsellor for salt
    and
A Madman to stir all up.

*–Abraham Hayward*

# Busha Browne's Spicy Bean Salad

Perfect for a tropical luncheon buffet as it can be made ahead,
is pretty and can be served to a large number of guests.

🌴

| | | |
|---|---|---|
| 2 cups | Dried red peas (kidney beans) | 500 ml |
| 1 cup | Dried gungo peas or black-eyed peas | 250 ml |
| 1 cup | Dried lentils | 250 ml |
| 1 cup | Steamed young green string beans, cut in ½"(1 cm) bits | 250 ml |
| 1 | Sweet onion, sliced thinly and separated into rings | 1 |
| 1 tbsp | Parsley, minced | 15 ml |
| ¼ cup | Red radishes, sliced | 60 ml |
| ½ | Green sweet pepper, sliced thinly | ½ |
| 2 cups | Great House Vinaigrette Dressing (see below) | 500 ml |
| ½ cup | ❖ Busha Browne's Spicy Tomato Love-Apple Sauce | 125 ml |

Soak dried peas overnight in cold water. Precook them separately, until
soft but still whole and firm. When cool, drain off water and place all
beans carefully in large earthenware bowl to avoid bruising. Add onions
and green pepper and pour over all 2 cups (500 ml) Great House
Viniagrette Dressing to which has been added the *Spicy Tomato Sauce*.
Cover tightly and refrigerate, preferably overnight, to allow marinade to
penetrate thoroughly. Makes about 2 quarts of salad.

# Great House Vinaigrette Dressing

A classic salad dressing which can also be used as a marinade.

🌴

| | | |
|---|---|---|
| ½ cup | Best quality herb vinegar | 125 ml |
| ½ cup | Left over dry red wine | 125 ml |
| 1 tbsp | ❖ Busha Browne's Spicy & Hot Pepper Sherry | 15 ml |
| 2 | Cloves garlic, crushed in a garlic press | 2 |
| 2 tbsp | Granulated sugar | 30 ml |
| ½ tsp | Celery salt | 2 ml |
| 1 tsp | Oregano (optional) | 5 ml |
| ¼ tsp | Freshly ground black pepper | 1 ml |
| 1 cup | Extra virgin olive oil | 250 ml |

Soak crushed garlic in herb vinegar and red wine. Stir in other ingredients
adding the oil last. Pour into a jar with a tight fitting lid and shake well.
Let ripen until ready to serve. (This dressing does not require refrigeration.)
Makes about 2 cups of dressing.

# Goblin Hill Ortanique Salad

An excellent and colourful addition to a party buffet table.

🌴

| | | |
|---|---|---|
| 2 | Large ripe tomatoes | 2 |
| 1 | Ripe sweet Jamaican ortanique, peeled | 1 |
| 1 | Small sweet onion, sliced thinly and separated into rings | 1 |
| ¼ cup | Fresh sweet basil leaves | 60 ml |
| | DRESSING | |
| ¼ cup | Herb vinegar | 60 ml |
| 1 tbsp | ❖ Busha Browne's Spicy & Hot Pepper Sherry | 15 ml |
| 1 tsp | Granulated sugar | 5 ml |
| | Juice of 1 clove garlic, crushed | |

Slice the tomatoes and the ortanique and arrange alternately with onion rings on a shallow platter. Rinse the basil leaves: dry and chop most of them, reserving some for garnish. Sprinkle the chopped bits over the tomato/ortanique/onion slices. Combine ingredients for the dressing and drizzle over the salad. Garnish with whole basil leaves. Serve on individual plates for a small dinner or on a platter for a buffet. Serves 4.

# Spicy Cucumber Slices–Chinese Style

🌴

| | | |
|---|---|---|
| 1 | Crisp fresh cucumber | 1 |
| 3 - 4 slices | Sweet onion, separated into rings | 3 - 4 |
| | DRESSING | |
| 1 tsp | Lime juice or | 5 ml |
| 1 tbsp | Spiced herb vinegar | 15 ml |
| 1 tsp | ❖ Busha Browne's Spicy & Hot Pepper Sherry | 5 ml |
| ½ tsp | Light brown sugar | 2 ml |
| ¼ tsp | Salt | 1 ml |
| ⅛ tsp | Freshly ground black pepper | 5 ml |
| | Juice of 1 clove garlic, crushed | |

Peel alternate lengthwise strips from cucumber, leaving 4 or 5 green stripes. Using a fork, score the cucumber lengthwise. With a sharp knife, slice thinly into a bowl. Add the onion rings. Mix all ingredients for dressing, and pour over cucumber and onion. Shake to cover the cucumber slices with the dressing: cover tightly and refrigerate for at least 1 hour. Will keep for several days, covered and refrigerated. Serves 2.

# Julienne of Avocado

Avocado or Alligator Pear as it is known in Jamaica, is highly regarded by the populace of the island. There are 'out of season' avocado pears but this fruit is generally available between August and October when breadfruit, its ubiquitous companion, is prevalent. Eaten with cassava bammy it is considered a particular culinary treat.

❦

| | | |
|---|:---:|---:|
| 1 | Small avocado | 1 |
| 1 tsp | Juice of lime or lemon | 5 ml |
| 1 tsp | ❖ Busha Browne's Original Spicy Planters Sauce | 5 ml |

Thinly slice avocado and peel, then arrange prettily on a plate, sprinkle with lime or lemon juice, and dot with the *Planters Sauce*. Cover tightly with plastic wrap until ready to serve. Serve avocado slices with toast triangles or on crackers. Serves 4.

# Yellowheart Breadfruit Salad

This salad can be made with Yellow Yam or Irish Potatoes. If using potatoes, new potatoes boiled in the skin (which is not removed) give the best flavour.

❦

| | | |
|---|:---:|---:|
| 1 | Medium sized boiled yellowheart breadfruit | 1 |
| | or | |
| 3 lb | Yellow yam (or Irish potatoes) | 1.5 kg |
| 1 | Onion, diced | 1 |
| 3 | Stalks escallion, using both white and green leaves, or chives, chopped | 3 |
| ¼ cup | Green sweet pepper, diced | 60 ml |
| | Salt to taste | |
| 1 tbsp | ❖ Busha Browne's Spicy & Hot Pepper Sherry | 15 ml |
| 1 cup | Busha Browne's Jiffy Mayonnaise (Page 81) | 250 ml |
| 2 | Hard-boiled eggs, chopped (optional) | 2 |
| 1 tbsp | Thinly sliced black olives (optional) | 15 ml |
| ¼ cup | Dry white wine or | 60 ml |
| ¼ cup | Milk | 60 ml |

Boil breadfruit, yam or potatoes until cooked but still firm. Cut into cubes while still hot. Add chopped onion, escallion or chives and green pepper.

Stir in the Busha Browne's Jiffy Mayonnaise, to which has been added the *Pepper Sherry*. If necessary, thin mixture with either ¼ cup (50 ml) of dry white wine or milk. Season to taste. Leave in covered bowl in refrigerator to chill for at least 24 hours. Serves 6.

# Milk River Spa Salad

🌴

| | | |
|---|---|---|
| ¼ cup | Toasted slivered almonds | 50 ml |
| 1 cup | Star Apple segments with milky juice | 250 ml |
| 1 cup | Thinly sliced cho-cho or zucchini | 250 ml |
| ¼ cup | Thinly sliced red radish | 60 ml |
| ¼ cup | Finely chopped green escallion tops or chives | 60 ml |
| | DRESSING | |
| ½ cup | Fresh pineapple juice | 125 ml |
| ½ cup | Concentrated chicken stock | 125 ml |
| ¼ cup | Lime or lemon juice | 60 ml |
| 1 tbsp | ❖ Busha Browne's Hot & Spicy Pepper Sherry | 15 ml |
| ½ tsp | Celery Salt | 2 ml |
| 2 tbsp | Light brown sugar | 30 ml |
| 2 tbsp | Extra virgin olive oil | 30 ml |

Place salad ingredients in bowl. Mix dressing ingredients in a screwtop jar, and shake well to blend. Add to salad and toss just before serving.

# Calico Cabbage

🌴

| | | |
|---|---|---|
| 2½ cups | Red Stripe Beer | 625 ml |
| ½ cup | Light brown sugar | 125 ml |
| 1½ cups each | Green and red cabbage, finely shredded (prepare in separate bowls, combine later) | each 375 ml |
| 1½ cups | Carrots, coarsely shredded | 375 ml |
| ½ cup | Sweet onion, minced | 125 ml |
| 1 cup | Plain unsweetened yogurt | 250 ml |
| ¼ cup | ❖ Busha Browne's Original Pepper Jelly | 60 ml |
| 1 tsp | Celery seed | 5 ml |
| 1 cup | Herb vinegar | 250 ml |
| ¼ cup | ❖ Busha Browne's Spicy & Hot Pepper Sherry | 60 ml |

Reserve ½ cup beer. Bring the rest to the boil with the sugar. Pour over cabbages which have been mixed with carrots and onions. Let stand one hour, then wring the cabbages 'dry' in a muslin bag with your hands. In a glass bowl combine the yogurt with the ½ cup reserved cold beer. Blend in the *Pepper Jelly*, the celery seed, vinegar and the *Pepper Sherry*. Add to vegetables and refrigerate overnight. Combine before serving. Serves 8.

# Green & Gold Salad with Spicy Paw Paw Dressing

Reminiscent of the green, gold and black flag of Jamaica, which is explained thus: 'Hardships there are, but the land is green, and the sun shineth.'

| | | |
|---|---|---|
| 2 cups | Ripe paw paw, peeled, seeded and cubed (reserve seeds) | 500 ml |
| 2 cups | Firm ripe avocado, peeled and cubed | 500 ml |
| 1 cup | Cucumber, thinly sliced | 250 ml |
| 1 | Purple onion, sliced in rings | 1 |
| 2-3 qt | Mixed lettuce in bite-sized pieces | 2-3 l |
| | DRESSING | |
| 1½ cups | White wine vinegar | 375 ml |
| 2 tbsp | ❖ Busha Browne's Spicy & Hot Pepper Sherry | 30 ml |
| 1 | Onion chopped | 1 |
| 1 | Garlic clove, minced | 1 |
| 1½ tsp | Salt | 7 ml |
| ½ tsp | Paprika | 2 ml |
| 1½ tsp | Dry mustard | 7 ml |
| ¾ cup | Granulated sugar | 180 ml |
| 3 cups | Vegetable oil | 750 ml |
| 3 tbsp | Fresh paw paw seeds | 40 ml |

Combine fruit, vegetables and lettuce in large earthenware bowl. In a blender, thoroughly combine vinegar, the *Pepper Sherry*, onion, spices and sugar. Gradually blend in oil, and then paw paw seeds. Blend until seeds are coarsely chopped. Toss salad with dressing and serve. Refrigerate remaining dressing until ready to use. Serves 6.

# Mock Asparagus

Since asparagus is not easily obtained in Jamaica, tender young callaloo stalks are an unusual and delicate substitute.

| | | |
|---|---|---|
| 1 lb | Callaloo | 500 g |
| ½ tsp | Salt | 2 ml |
| ⅛ tsp | Freshly ground black pepper | .5 ml |

Remove leaves from the callaloo, and reserve for another dish. Strip skin off the stems and cut them into 5 in (12 cm) lengths. Steam until tender. Serve callaloo stems hot or cold with Busha Browne's Spicy Cheese Sauce or Busha's Hollandaise Sauce (page 80).

# Busha Browne's Stuffed Love-Apples

🌴

| | | |
|---|---|---|
| 4 | Large firm red tomatoes | 4 |
| 2 | Small onions, minced | 2 |
| 2 | Garlic cloves, put through press | 2 |
| 1 tbsp | Olive oil | 15 ml |
| 1 cup | Cooked aubergine | 250 ml |
| 2 tbsp | Parsley or cilantro, chopped | 30 ml |
| ¼ cup | Thinly sliced water chestnuts (optional) | 60 ml |
| 1 cup | Cooked brown rice or bulgur | 250 ml |
| ¼ cup | ❖ Busha Browne's Spicy Tomato Love-Apple Sauce | 60 ml |
| ¼ cup | Grated cheddar cheese | 60 ml |
| | Fresh basil leaves | |

Slice tops from tomatoes, scoop out insides with juice and set aside. Sauté onion and garlic in olive oil. Add aubergine, tomato pulp, parsley, and water chestnuts. Sauté 2–3 minutes. Add cooked rice or bulgur and Spicy Tomato Sauce. Stir gently to mix. Spoon into tomato cases. Sprinkle with grated cheese and place under grill for 2–3 minutes until the cheese is browned. Turn off the broiler and allow to sit for 5 minutes. Garnish with fresh basil leaves and serve. Serves 4.

# Sweet & Sour Beets

🌴

| | | |
|---|---|---|
| 3 cups | Freshly cooked beets, sliced | 750 ml |
| ½ cup | Light brown sugar | 125 ml |
| 1 tbsp | Cornstarch | 15 ml |
| ½ tsp | Salt | 2 ml |
| 3 | Whole cloves | 3 |
| 3 | Whole pimento seeds | 3 |
| ½ cup | Herb vinegar | 125 ml |
| 1 tbsp | ❖ Busha Browne's Spicy & Hot Pepper Sherry | 15 ml |
| 2 tbsp | Unsalted butter | 30 ml |
| 2 tbsp | ❖ Busha Browne's Burned Orange Marmalade | 30 ml |

Mix together the sugar, cornstarch, salt, cloves, pimento, vinegar and Pepper Sherry and cook them in the top of a double boiler over direct heat until the mixture thickens and becomes clear. Add the beets and keep all warm over hot water. Just before serving, reheat and add the butter and the Marmalade while stirring carefully. Serves 4.

# Garden Egg Creole

In Jamaica aubergine or eggplant is referred to as Garden Egg

🌴 🌴

| | | |
|---|---|---|
| 2 tbsp | Olive Oil | 30 ml |
| 4 | Cloves garlic, bruised | 4 |
| 2 | Medium size onions, sliced thinly | 2 |
| 1 cup | Okra, sliced | 250 ml |
| 1 | Sweet green pepper, julienne | 1 |
| 1 lb | Zucchini, sliced ¼ in (5 mm) thick | 500 g |
| 2 lb | Aubergine, diced and drained | 1 kg |
| 2 tbsp | ❖ Busha Browne's Original Spicy Planters Sauce | 30 ml |
| 1 tsp | ❖ Busha Browne's Pukka Hot Pepper Sauce | 5 ml |
| 1½ cups | Stewed plum tomatoes | 375 ml |
| 1 tbsp | ❖ Busha Browne's Hot & Spicy Pepper Sherry | 15 ml |
| 6 oz | Prepared tomato paste | 180 g |
| 1 cup | Boiling water | 250 ml |
| ¼ cup | Cornstarch | 60 ml |
| | Cold water | |
| | Salt and pepper to taste | |
| 1 cup | Dried breadcrumbs | 250 ml |
| 2 oz | Grated cheese | 60 g |
| 4 | Black olives, in slivers | 4 |
| 2 | Rashers crisp bacon, finely diced (optional) | 2 |

Heat oil in a large, deep saucepan. Add garlic and remove before it burns. Add the onions and stir until golden. Add in order, the okra, sweet peppers and zucchini stirring constantly. Add aubergine, *Busha Browne's Sauces* and diced stewed tomatoes. Continue cooking, stirring constantly until vegetables produce enough liquid to allow them to cook without burning. Cover tightly, reduce heat, and simmer over low heat 35-45 minutes. Mix tomato paste with cup of boiling water. Dissolve cornstarch in sufficient cold water to make a thin paste and add to hot tomato paste liquid. Pour slowly into vegetables, stirring constantly until mixture has come together and thickened. Correct seasoning. Fill ovenproof casserole and refrigerate for at least 24 hours. Remove from refrigerator, and sprinkle with breadcrumbs. Garnish with grated cheese and olives or crisp bacon bits, if desired. Bake for about 30 minutes at 350° F (180° C) or until heated through. May also be served cold. Serves 8.

TIP: *This recipe is improved by remaining refrigerated for 2-3 days and is perfect for a vegetarian meal or as an accompaniment for a luncheon buffet table.*

VARIATION: *For added interest include ½ cup chopped unsalted peanuts.*

# Princess Street Vegetable Stirfry

A superlative vegetarian dish for a special dinner party.
Princess Street was originally the heart of Kingston's thriving
Chinatown and the site of its most famous Chinese restaurant.

| | | |
|---|---|---|
| 2 tbsp | Best quality vegetable oil | 30 ml |
| 1 in | Fresh Ginger root peeled and crushed (optional) | 2.5 cm |
| 2 cloves | Garlic cloves, peeled and bruised | 2 |
| ½ tsp | Salt | 2 ml |
| | Selection of at least six of the following vegetables: | |
| 1 | Large onion, sliced lengthwise separated to resemble flower petals | 1 |
| ½ cup | Cauliflower or broccoli flowerets | 125 ml |
| ½ cup | Snow Peas | 125 ml |
| ½ cup | Carrots, julienne | 125 ml |
| ½ cup | Fresh mushrooms, sliced | 125 ml |
| ½ cup | Celery, cut in ½ (1 cm) chunks | 125 ml |
| ½ cup | Cho-cho, sliced thinly | 125 ml |
| ½ cup | Chopped escallion | 125 ml |
| ½ cup | Bamboo shoots | 125 ml |
| 1 cup | Bean sprouts | 250 ml |
| 1 cup | Zucchini, julienne | 250 ml |
| 1 cup | Coarsely chopped cabbage | 250 ml |
| 1 cup | Coarsely chopped pak choy | 250 ml |
| ½ cup | Water chestnuts, sliced | 125 ml |
| 1 tsp | Soy sauce | 5 ml |
| 1 tbsp | ❖ Busha Browne's Spicy & Hot Pepper Sherry | 15 ml |
| 2 tbsp | ❖ Busha Browne's Original Spicy Planters Sauce | 30 ml |
| 2 tbsp | ❖ Busha Browne's Ginger Pepper Jelly | 30 ml |
| 2 tbsp | Toasted sunflower seeds | 60 g |

Heat oil in wok or skillet. When hot add garlic and ginger and toss until
the fragrance rises, then remove and discard. Add the salt, then the
vegetables one at a time, stirring continually. Start with hard vegetables,
introducing leafy vegetables last. When all are slightly wilted but still
crisp, sprinkle on the soy sauce, the *Pepper Sherry* and the *Planters Sauce*.
Melt the *Pepper Jelly* in a little water, stir into the vegetables, and add
sunflower seeds. Cover to steam for about 5 minutes. Serve immediately,
straight from the wok. Serves 6-8.

VARIATION: *Cashew nuts may be used as an alternative to water chestnuts.*

TIP: *Dish is best with inclusion of equal mixtures of hard and soft vegetables.*

# Llandovery Callaloo Timbale

Llandovery, one of Jamaica's oldest sugar estates, has been in
continuous production since 1674. The mark on the rum
puncheons, TTL, stood for Thomas Townsend, Llandovery,
and was regarded as a guarantee of a premium quality rum.

🌴

| | | |
|---|---|---|
| 1 cup | Busha Browne's Classic Béchamel Sauce (page 80) | 250ml |
| 2 cups | Steamed, drained, finely chopped callaloo | 500 ml |
| 3 | Beaten eggs | 3 |
| ½ cup | Grated sharp cheese (optional) | 125 ml |
| ¼ cup | Concentrated chicken stock | 60 ml |
| 1 tbsp | ❖ Busha Browne's Original Spicy Planters Sauce | 15 ml |
| 1 tbsp | Premium Jamaican gold rum | 15 ml |
| | Salt and pepper | |
| | Freshly grated nutmeg | |

Grease a ring mould or 6 individual ovenproof ramekins. Prepare the
Béchamel sauce. While still warm, add the drained, chopped callaloo.
Add the beaten eggs, cheese (if used), stock, rum, the seasonings and the
*Planters Sauce*, folding them in gently. Turn into the greased mould, and
place in a larger roasting pan. Add hot water to come halfway up the
mould, and then place in oven preheated to 325° F (160° C) for 45
minutes or until set and a knife inserted halfway between the edge and the
centre of the timbale comes out clean. To unmould, run a knife around
the edge. This dish can be served warm or cold. Fill the centre of the ring
with a colourful combination of steamed, well drained diced vegetables.
Garnish as desired with or without Busha's Hollandaise Sauce (page 80).
An elegant dish for a buffet party. Serves 6.

# Pukka Pumpkin Curry

🌴 🌴

| | | |
|---|---|---|
| 1 | Small dry calabaza pumpkin | 1 |
| 1 tbsp | Butter | 15 ml |
| 1 tsp | ❖ Busha Browne's Original Spicy Planters Sauce | 15 ml |
| ½ tsp | ❖ Busha Browne's Pukka Hot Pepper Sauce | 2 ml |
| ½ tsp | Best Indian curry powder | 2 ml |

Cut pumpkin in halves and take out seeds and strings. Do not peel. Steam
until cooked. Remove hard skin. Crush with butter and *Planters Sauce* and
*Pukka Sauce*. Add curry powder and whip until creamy. If too thick, use
a little milk or chicken stock to thin. Serves 4.

# Planter's Stuffed Green Paw Paw

🌴 🌴

| 3 | Small green paw paws | 3 |
|---|---|---|
| | Salt | |
| ½ cup | Onion, minced | 125 ml |
| 3 tbsp | Butter | 40 ml |
| 1 cup | Fresh corn, cut off the cob | 250 ml |
| ¼ cup | Unsalted cashew nuts, chopped | 60 ml |
| 2 tbsp | ❖ Busha Browne's Original Spicy Planters Sauce | 30 ml |
| ¼ tsp | ❖ Busha Browne's Pukka Hot Pepper Sauce | 1 ml |
| ¼ cup | Dried breadcrumbs | 60 ml |
| 3 tbsp | Cheddar Cheese, grated | 40 ml |
| 2 | Rashers crisp bacon crumbled (optional) | 2 |

Cut green paw paws in half lengthwise and remove seeds. Drop into boiling, salted water and cook until tender. Drain and cool. Remove pulp and reserve, leaving shells to be stuffed.

In a skillet, lightly sauté the onion in melted butter. Add corn, cashew nuts, *Busha Browne's sauces* and paw paw pulp. Spoon mixture into paw paw shells, sprinkle with bread crumbs, cheese and bacon bits. Place under hot grill briefly until cheese bubbles and is golden brown. Serves 6.

# Busha's Fancy Sweet Potatoes

🌴

| 4 | Medium sized sweet potatoes | 4 |
|---|---|---|
| ¼ cup | Butter | 60 ml |
| ½ cup | Dark brown sugar | 125 ml |
| ½ tsp | Salt | 2 ml |
| 1 cup | Red Stripe Beer | 250 ml |
| 2 tbsp | ❖ Busha Browne's Spicy & Hot Pepper Sherry | 30 ml |
| 2 tbsp | ❖ Busha Browne's Burned Orange Marmalade | 30 ml |

Peel the raw sweet potatoes, and cut them crosswise into ½ inch (1.5 cm) slices. Melt butter and sugar together in a heavy deep skillet until quite brown. Add salt and beer, stirring constantly until all sugar is dissolved.

Drop sweet potato slices into the boiling syrup, and cook over medium heat for 15 minutes. Add the *Pepper Sherry*, and the *Marmalade* and cook for a further 15 minutes. Place slices in serving dish and pour syrup over them. Reheat in oven. Serves 6.

# Sligo Mushrooms & Pepper Sherry

🌴

| | | |
|---|---|---|
| 2 cups | Fresh mushrooms, sliced | 500 ml |
| 2-3 | Chopped shallots | 2-3 |
| 2 tbsp | ❖ Busha Browne's Spicy & Hot Pepper Sherry | 30 ml |
| 1 tbsp | Unsalted butter | 15 ml |
| | Salt and freshly ground black pepper to taste | |

Sauté shallots in melted butter. Add mushrooms and the *Pepper Sherry*. Simmer slowly until tender. Do not overcook. Season with salt and pepper. Serve immediately on crisp toast. Serves 4.

# Spicy Snow Peas & Mushrooms

🌴

| | | |
|---|---|---|
| 2 cups | Fresh young green snow peas | 500 ml |
| 1 cup | Fresh mushrooms, sliced | 250 ml |
| 2 | Shallots, chopped | 2 |
| 1 | Clove garlic, crushed | 1 |
| 1 tbsp | Soy sauce (optional) | 15 ml |
| 2 tbsp | ❖ Busha Browne's Spicy & Hot Pepper Sherry | 30 ml |
| 1 tbsp | Extra-virgin olive oil | 15 ml |

Heat oil in skillet and add garlic. Add the shallots and sauté lightly. Introduce snow peas and mushrooms, stirring often. Add soy sauce and the *Pepper Sherry*. Do not overcook. Serve promptly. Serves 4.

# Busha's Spicy Glazed Onions

🌴

| | | |
|---|---|---|
| 1 lb | Small round onions, peeled | 500 g |
| 4 tbsp | Butter | 60 ml |
| 4 tbsp | ❖ Busha Browne's Ginger Pepper Jelly | 60 ml |

Cook onions covered until tender. Drain and place in shallow buttered baking dish. Melt butter and the *Pepper Jelly* together. Pour over onions and heat under grill for a few minutes. Serves 4.

VARIATION: *Other vegetables such as carrots, beets, turnips, Jerusalem artichokes and endives may be glazed in the same way.*

# Sandwiches
## &
# Picnic Snacks

The sandwich was reputed to have been invented by the fourth Earl of Sandwich who was so addicted to gambling that he refused to take time out to eat a meal. One solemn moment in 1762 when hunger was getting the better of the Earl's desire, he roared to a waiter for two pieces of bread, slapped his beefsteak between them, and the sandwich was born.

# Summer Salad Sandwiches

🌴

| | | |
|---|---|---|
| 1 cup | Cooked, cooled chicken, finely chopped | 250 ml |
| 1 | Small onion, diced | 1 |
| ¼ cup | Chopped celery | 60 ml |
| 1 tbsp | Busha Browne's Jiffy Mayonnaise (page 81) | 15 ml |
| 1 tbsp | ❖ Busha Browne's Original Spicy Planters Sauce | 15 ml |
| | Salt and pepper to taste | |
| 4 | Round sesame seed buns or | 4 |
| | English Muffins | |
| 3 tbsp | Chopped cashew nuts or walnuts | 40 ml |
| | ❖ Busha Browne's Spicy Fruit Chutney | |

Mix together chicken, onion, celery, Jiffy Mayonnaise and *Planters Sauce*. Season to taste. Split and toast buns then butter while hot and top each side with chicken mixture. Serve open, sprinkled with chopped nutmeats and garnished with parsley and celery stalks with *Busha Browne's Spicy Fruit Chutney* on the side. Serves 4.

# Busha Browne's Egg Sandwiches

🌴 🌴

| | | |
|---|---|---|
| 2 | Hard-boiled eggs, crushed | 2 |
| ¼ cup | Finely chopped escallion (use both white and green) | 60 ml |
| 1 tbsp | Bombay Curry Mayonnaise (page 81) | 15 ml |
| | or | |
| 1 tsp | Soft Butter | 5 ml |
| 1 tbsp | Milk | 15 ml |
| 1 tsp | ❖ Busha Browne's Original Spicy Planters Sauce | 5 ml |
| ⅛ tsp | ❖ Busha Browne's Pukka Hot Pepper Sauce | .5 ml |
| ¼ tsp | Dry mustard | 1 ml |
| | Salt and pepper to taste | |
| 8 slices | Wholewheat bread | 8 slices |

Mix crushed eggs with chopped escallion, Jiffy Mayonnaise and/or butter and milk until it is creamy enough to spread. Add *Planters Sauce*, *Pukka Sauce*, dry mustard, and salt and pepper to taste. Spread on bread and top with second slice. Garnish with alfalfa sprouts. Makes 4 sandwiches.

# Alligator Pear Sandwiches

| | | |
|---|---|---|
| 1 | Small avocado | 1 |
| 2 tbsp | ❖ Busha Browne's Original Spicy Planters Sauce | 30 ml |
| ½ tsp | Lime or lemon juice | 2 ml |
| 4 slices | Hard-dough bread | |

Crush peeled avocado lightly with *Planters Sauce* and lime or lemon juice to prevent discolouration. Serve on toasted sliced buttered hard-dough bread, either covered or open, cut into fingers.

# Cucumber Sandwiches

This is a traditional English teatime sandwich, and is often served in Jamaica where many people still enjoy the ritual of teatime at 4:00 or 5:00 in the afternoon.

| | | |
|---|---|---|
| 1 | Firm cucumber | 1 |
| 1 tbsp | ❖ Busha Browne's Spicy & Hot Pepper Sherry | 15 ml |
| 8 slices | White or brown bread, sliced thinly | 8 slices |

Score and thinly slice a firm cucumber. Marinate for at least ½ hour in *Busha Browne's Spicy & Hot Pepper Sherry*. Butter thin slices of fresh white bread and remove the crusts. Blot the slices of cucumber on a paper towel, then place on buttered bread, top with second slice of buttered bread. Slice off crusts and cut each sandwich in quarters and garnish.

# Busha Browne's Swanky Franky

---

Frankfurters as needed
An equal number of cheese slices
Rashers of bacon
❖ Busha Browne's Spicy Tomato Love-Apple Sauce
Vienna rolls

---

Split frankfurters, and stuff with slice of cheese. Wrap with a slice of bacon, secure with a toothpick. Put under the grill until bacon is cooked. Place in warmed roll and top with *Spicy Tomato Sauce*.

# Pukka Cheese & Chutney Sandwiches

### 🌴 🌴

---

*Freshly baked sesame seed rolls*
*Butter*
*Sliced Cheddar Cheese*
❖ *Busha Browne's Spicy Fruit or Banana Chutney*
❖ *Busha Browne's Pukka Hot Pepper Sauce*

---

Split sesame rolls and butter. Fill with sliced cheese topped with chutney into which has been mixed a dash of *Pukka Sauce*. Garnish with salad greens, alfalfa sprouts or crudités.
VARIATION: *May be used as an open sandwich toasted under the grill until the cheese melts.*

# Toasted Pepper Jelly Sandwiches
Ideal as a snack or at teatime.

###

---

*White, brown or rye bread*
*Butter*
❖ *Busha Browne's Original Pepper Jelly*

---

Toast thinly sliced bread (homemade German type or rye bread is best) and butter immediately while hot. Pile on the *Pepper Jelly*. Spread jelly thinly and cut into fingers if serving at teatime.
VARIATION: *Also delicious including peanut butter or cheese.*

# Spinnaker Sandwiches
A favourite treat for the spinnaker crew because these sandwiches are easily handled on the deck of a yacht.

---

*White or brown bread*
*Butter (optional)*
*Peanut butter*
❖ *Busha Browne's Twice-Boiled Guava Jelly*

---

Butter both sides of sandwiches if desired. Spread each slice with peanut butter topped with the *Guava Jelly*. 'Paste' together in pairs. Jelly should not run out at the sides if made this way.

# Busha Browne's Fish Pockets

| 2 | Pita breads | 2 |
|---|---|---|
| 1 lb | Freshly cooked fillet of Albacore or Salmon | 500 g |
| | Chopped onion (optional) | |
| | Chopped celery | |
| 1 tbsp | Green Island Mayonnaise (page 81) | 15 ml |
| | or plain unsweetened yogurt | |
| 1 tsp | ❖ Busha Browne's Original Spicy Planters Sauce | 5 ml |
| 1 tsp | ❖ Busha Browne's Spicy Tomato Love-Apple Sauce | 5 ml |
| | Lettuce or alfalfa sprouts | |

Flake the fish. Chop the onion and celery and mix together with the mayonnaise, the *Planters Sauce* and the *Spicy Tomato Sauce*. Cut pita bread pockets in half, and split layers. Put filling into pockets and top with lettuce or alfalfa sprouts. Wrap well individually in plastic wrap and chill. Excellent with *Busha Browne's Spicy Fruit Chutney*. Serves 4.
VARIATION: *As an alternative to freshly cooked fish, use best quality tuna, smoked marlin or an equal quantity of cooked, chopped chicken meat.*

## Roasted Meat Sandwiches

Spread fresh bread or toast with butter and/or mayonnaise as preferred. Top with cold roast beef, roast pork or veal, dotted with *Busha Browne's Original Spicy Planter's Sauce* and/or *Busha Browne's Pukka Hot Pepper Sauce* if desired. Add lettuce or alfalfa sprouts. Top with second slice of bread or toast. Secure with toothpicks and serve with *Busha Browne's Spicy Fruit Chutney* or *Busha Browne's Original Pepper Jelly* on the side.

## Devilled Ham Sandwiches

Chop finely left-over bits of baked ham. Add enough Busha Browne's Jiffy Mayonnaise or plain unsweetened yogurt to bind together. Blend in a dash or two of *Busha Browne's Pukka Hot Pepper Sauce* and *Busha Browne's Original Spicy Planters Sauce* to taste. Make into sandwiches and serve with alfalfa sprouts and *Busha Browne's Original Banana Chutney* or any of the three *Pepper Jellies* on the side.

# Busha Browne's Variations on Picnics

## Castleton Weiners

Generations of Jamaican children remember visiting Castleton
Botanical Gardens, in the hills of St Andrew, and improvising
tasty picnic snacks which they would cook for themselves on
a coal pot set on the banks of the Wagwater River.

| 12 | Best quality weiners | 12 |
|---|---|---|
| 12 | Split buttered Vienna rolls | 12 |
| | ❖ Busha Browne's Spicy Tomato Love-Apple Sauce | |

Steam weiners in boiling water until hot. Pack into a wide-mouth
insulated flask and fill with boiling water. Cover and pack. When ready
to eat, heat buttered rolls over barbecue, then combine with weiners.
Spread *Spicy Tomato Sauce* over weiners and serve.

## Marinated Picnic Chicken

| 3 lb | Chicken, cut into serving pieces | 1.5 kg |
|---|---|---|
| 2 tbsp | ❖ Busha Browne's Spicy Jerk Sauce | 30 ml |
| 1 tbsp | Olive oil | 15 ml |
| ¼ cup | Stone ground yellow cornmeal | 60 ml |
| | ❖ Busha Browne's Original Spicy Planters Sauce | |

Mix the *Spicy Jerk Sauce*, olive oil and cornmeal together to make a paste.
Rub well into chicken pieces and refrigerate overnight in airtight container.
Carry to the picnic site in an ice chest and cook over barbecue.

## Spicy Corn-on-the-Cob

| 4 | Fresh sweet corn cobs | 4 |
|---|---|---|
| 2 qts | Water | 2 l |
| ½ tsp | ❖ Busha Browne's Spicy Jerk Sauce | 2 ml |
| 1 tsp | ❖ Busha Browne's Spicy & Hot Pepper Sherry | 5 ml |
| 1 tsp | Light brown sugar | 5 ml |
| 1 tbsp | Butter | 15 ml |

Add *Busha Browne's Sauces*, sugar and butter to cold water. Cover and
bring to the boil. Add the corn cobs. Boil for 3 minutes only, cover and
leave to cool. Pack in a wide-mouthed insulated flask and fill with the
reheated spiced water. Serve from flask with additional butter and salt.

# Fish
## &
# Crustaceans

"Up in the Hills, where the streams are cool,
And Mullet and Jonga swim in the pool,
I have ten acres of mountainside,
An' a dainty-foot donkey that I ride."

—*Song of the Banana Man*
*Evan Jones*

# Busha's Stuffed Baked Snapper

🌴

| 2 lb | Fresh whole Snapper or other fish | 1 kg |
|---|---|---|
| 2 tbsp | Lime or lemon juice | 30 ml |
| | Salt and pepper to taste | |
| 1 tbsp | Butter for basting | 15 ml |
| | Sliced limes or lemons and sprigs of parsley for garnish | |
| | STUFFING | |
| ½ | Small onion, finely chopped | ½ |
| 1 | Small tomato, chopped | 1 |
| 1 tbsp | Melted butter or best quality oil | 15 ml |
| 1 tsp | ❖ Busha Browne's Original Spicy Planters Sauce | 5 ml |
| 1 tsp | ❖ Busha Browne's Spicy & Hot Pepper Sherry | 5 ml |
| ½ cup | Concentrated chicken or fish stock | 125 ml |
| ½ cup | Dried breadcrumbs | 125 ml |

Wash scaled fish after trimming fins. Squeeze lime juice over and inside fish, then sprinkle with salt and pepper. Place in covered dish in refrigerator and prepare stuffing. Sauté onion and tomato in melted butter or oil until soft, then add the *Planters Sauce*, the *Pepper Sherry* and stock. Stir until heated through. Add breadcrumbs and continue cooking at a low temperature until mixture holds together. Stuff mixture into body cavity of fish, closing opening with toothpicks around which string is wound. Put a small pat of butter on top and bake in 350°F (180°C) oven until cooked. Be careful not to overcook. Serve on heated platter and garnish with slices of lime or lemon and parsley sprigs. Serves 4.

# Savoury Sweet Potato Stuffing

🌴 🌴

| 1½ lb | Sweet potato, boiled and crushed | 750 g |
|---|---|---|
| 1 | Small tomato, chopped | 1 |
| 1 | Medium onion, chopped | 1 |
| ½ cup | Butter | 125 ml |
| 1 tbsp | ❖ Busha Browne's Original Spicy Planters Sauce | 15 ml |
| Dash | ❖ Busha Browne's Pukka Hot Pepper Sauce | Dash |

Combine ingredients as above (no breadcrumbs required) and stuff fish. VARIATION: *Breadfruit or yellow yam may be substituted for sweet potato. Bake any left over stuffing in a ramekin when baking the fish.*

# Poached Snapper & Callaloo Sauce

🌴 🌴

| | | |
|---|---|---|
| 2 lb | Fresh fillet of Snapper or other white fish | 1 kg |
| 2 tsp | Lime or lemon juice | 10 ml |
| ¼ cup | Butter (2 ozs) | 60 ml |
| ¾ cup | Dry white wine | 180 ml |
| ¼ cup | ❖ Busha Browne's Spicy & Hot Pepper Sherry | 60 ml |
| 1 tbsp | Chopped escallion | 15 ml |
| ¼ cup | Fresh dill weed, chopped | 60 ml |
| ½ tsp | Salt and freshly ground pepper to taste | 2 ml |
| | SAUCE | 1cup |
| 1 cup | Busha Browne's Classic Béchamel Sauce (page 80 ) | 250 ml |
| 1cup | Callaloo or spinach, steamed and drained | 250 ml |
| 1 tsp | ❖ Busha Browne's Original Spicy Planters Sauce | 5 ml |

Squeeze lime juice over prepared fish. Melt butter in suitable pan, add white wine and *Pepper Sherry*, escallion and dill weed. Bring to a boil. Season with salt, and reduce heat to gentle simmer. Add fish. Poach fish fillets for 3 to 5 minutes and remove carefully. Keep warm.

SAUCE: Reduce poaching liquid to half by rapid boiling, then add Béchamel Sauce, steamed callaloo and the *Planters Sauce*. Place in blender and process until smooth. Place the warm poached fish on appropriate hot platter, cover with reheated sauce and garnish. Serves 6.

# Poached Kingfish & Mushrooms

🌴

| | | |
|---|---|---|
| 6 | Fresh fillets of Kingfish | 6 |
| 1 tbsp | Lime or lemon juice | 15 ml |
| 1 cup | Red Stripe Beer | 250 ml |
| ½ cup | Green escallion tops, finely chopped | 125 ml |
| 1 cup | Fresh mushrooms, sliced | 250 ml |
| ½ tsp | Celery salt | 2 ml |
| ½ tsp | Freshly ground black pepper | 2 ml |
| 1 tsp | ❖ Busha Browne's Original Spicy Planters Sauce | 5 ml |

Prepare as above and poach fish briefly. Reduce liquid, add mushrooms and correct seasoning. Pour over fish. Serve with *Planters Sauce*.

VARIATION: *Snow peas may be used instead of or in addition to mushrooms.*

# Escoveitched Fish Port Royal Style

Port Royal was known for three decades as 'The Wickedest City in the World', prior to its destruction in the great earthquake of 1692. The romance of this sunken city has fascinated archaeologists for centuries.

🌴 🌴 🌴

| | | |
|---|---|---|
| 2 lb | Kingfish or Snapper steaks, sliced ½" (1.3 cm) thick | 1 kg |
| 2 tbsp | Lime or lemon juice | 30 ml |
| | Best quality oil for frying | |
| | Salt and pepper | |
| 1 tbsp | Brown Sugar | 15 ml |
| 1½ cups | White cane vinegar | 375 ml |
| 1 tsp | ❖ Busha Browne's Pukka Hot Pepper Sauce | 5 ml |
| ½ cup | ❖ Busha Browne's Spicy & Hot Pepper Sherry | 125 ml |
| 1 | Large onion sliced thickly | 1 |
| ⅓ cup | Carrots, julienne | 80 ml |
| 8 | Whole pimento berries (allspice) | 8 |
| | Parsley and sweet red pepper slices for garnish | |

Wash prepared fish with lime juice. Dry fish thoroughly and season with salt and pepper. Heat oil and fry fish slices on both sides until crisp and brown. Place fish in a deep dish and set aside.

In a saucepan combine sugar, vinegar, *Pukka Sauce*, sliced onion, carrot and pimento berries. Bring to a rolling boil. Simmer until onion slices are tender. Remove from heat, add the *Pepper Sherry* and pour over fish. Marinate overnight. For breakfast, as an appetizer or a light luncheon dish serve cold with fried cassava bammy or hard-dough bread, lettuce and tomato slices. Serves 4.

TIP: *For a cocktail party, cut fish into 1 inch (2.5 cm) square bits and serve on toothpicks with Busha Browne's Spicy Cocktail Dip (page 15).*

# Pukka Grilled Fish

🌴 🌴 🌴

| | | |
|---|---|---|
| 4 | Small whole fish | 4 |
| | Fresh lime or lemon juice | |
| ½ tsp | ❖ Busha Browne's Pukka Hot Pepper Sauce | 2 ml |
| ½ cup | Flour, with salt and pepper added | 125 ml |

Mix lime juice and the *Pukka Sauce*. Rub fish with the mixture, inside and out. Dredge with flour to which salt and pepper has been added. Grill fish. Serve immediately. Best with lightly sautéed onions and *Love-Apple Sauce*.

# Busha Browne's Sherried Fish Fritters

🌴 🌴

| | | |
|---|---|---:|
| 1 lb | Fresh fish fillets | 500 g |
| 1 oz each | Onion, celery, red and green | 30 g |
| | sweet pepper, all diced finely | |
| 2 tbsp | Dark Jamaican rum or sherry | 30 ml |
| 1 tbsp | ❖ Busha Browne's Spicy & Hot Pepper Sherry | 15 ml |
| 1 tbsp | Cold water | 15 ml |
| | BATTER | |
| 1 | Whole egg | 1 |
| 1 tsp | ❖ Busha Browne's Spicy Tomato Love-Apple Sauce | 5 ml |
| ½ tsp | ❖ Busha Browne's Pukka Hot Pepper Sauce | 2 ml |
| ¼ tsp | Dried thyme | 1 ml |
| 2 cups | All purpose flour (8 ozs) | 500 ml |
| 1 tsp | Baking powder | |
| | Salt to taste | |
| | Water to mix | |
| | Best quality oil for deep frying | |
| | SAUCE | |
| 1 cup | Busha Browne's Jiffy Mayonnaise (page 81) | 250 ml |
| ¼ cup | Skimmed milk | 60 ml |
| 2 tbsp | Escallion, minced | 30 ml |
| 2 tbsp | Parsley, minced | 30 ml |
| 1 tbsp | Lemon juice | 15 ml |
| 2 tsp | Dried dillweed | 10 ml |
| ¼ tsp | Salt | 1 ml |
| ¼ tsp | ❖ Busha Browne's Pukka Hot Pepper Sauce | 1 ml |

Bring the rum and/or sherries to the boil with the water. Add the fish in batches and cook for 2 minutes. Drain the fish fillets and allow them to cool for ½ hour in the refrigerator.

BATTER: Mix the egg, flour, baking powder, Spicy Tomato Sauce, the Pukka Sauce and thyme with sufficient water to form a firm batter. Add fish, flaked finely and allow to rest for 20 minutes before deep frying. Use a dessertspoon for fritter size. Drop batter by spoonfuls into hot oil and fry until golden brown, then drain on paper towels.

Serve with SAUCE made by combining all the listed ingredients which have been chilled in a covered dish. Serves 4.

VARIATION: Can also be served with Busha Browne's Lime Pepper Jelly.

# Port Henderson Black Crab

These land crabs were once very common in the West Indies. It is said that, at breeding time these land crabs walk straight to the sea, in a direct line over anything in their path. They are sometimes kept alive for several days before being cooked, and are fed on pepper leaves and cornmeal to cleanse and flavour them. Sea crabs may be substituted.

🌴 🌴

| | | |
|---|---|---|
| 6 | Black Crabs boiled, to yield | 6 |
| 1 cup | Crab meat | 250 ml |
| 2 tbsp | Softened butter | 30 ml |
| 1 tsp | ❖ Busha Browne's Original Spicy Planters Sauce | 5 ml |
| ¼ tsp | ❖ Busha Browne's Pukka Hot Pepper Sauce | 1 ml |
| ¼ tsp | Freshly ground black pepper | 1 ml |
| 1 tbsp | Finely minced onion | 15 ml |
| 1 tsp | Lime or lemon juice | 5 ml |
| ½ tsp | Salt | 2 ml |
| | Breadcrumbs and butter for topping | |

Clean and pick out all the meat from the freshly cooked crabs, including claws and tentacles and shred. Save 4 good shells.

Lightly sauté onion and mix with crabmeat, butter, *Busha Browne's Sauces*, seasonings and lime juice. Do not allow mixture to become soggy. Wash the shells, and brush with oil. Fill with crab mixture, top with fresh breadcrumbs and dot with butter.

Preheat oven to 400° F (200° C) and bake for about 15-20 minutes or until heated through and crumbs become crisp and brown. Garnish with slices of lime and parsley sprigs. Serves 4.

TIP: *If hotter crabs are desired, increase amount of Busha Browne's Pukka Hot Pepper Sauce. It is customary to leave in the black eyes of the crabs when they are very hot and to remove the eyes if they are only mildly hot.*

# Lime 'N' Lobster

🌴

| | | |
|---|---|---|
| 2 | Fresh spiny lobsters about 1 lb (500 grs) each | 2 |
| 2 tbsp | Fresh lime juice | 30 ml |
| 2 tbsp | Melted butter | 30 ml |
| 2 tbsp | ❖ Busha Browne's Lime Pepper Jelly | 30 ml |

Split lobsters lengthwise and squeeze lime juice over them. Place under hot grill and cook until golden, brushing at intervals with *Busha Browne's Lime Pepper Jelly* and melted butter. Serve with additional butter and *Busha Browne's Lime Pepper Jelly*. Serves 2.

# Pedro Cays Sherried Lobster

### 🌴 🌴 🌴

| 2 | Fresh spiny lobsters, using meat and shells | 2 |
|---|---|---|
| ½ cup | Soy sauce | 125 ml |
| ½ cup | Best Spanish sherry | 125 ml |
| ½ cup | ❖ Busha Browne's Spicy & Hot Pepper Sherry | 125 ml |
| ¼ tsp | ❖ Busha Browne's Pukka Hot Pepper Sauce | 1 ml |
| 2 tbsp | Oil or melted butter | 30 ml |

Mix together soy sauce, sherry, *Pepper Sherry* and *Pukka Sauce*. Cut lobster meat into pieces, marinate in the mixture for at least 1 hour. Drain and place on a flat baking tin. Brush lobster meat with oil and grill for 10 minutes, about 3 inches (8 cm) from flame, basting frequently with the marinade. Place the lobster meat in the shells, baste generously with the marinade. Grill for 2 or 3 minutes more. Serve at once. Serves 4.

# Busha's Shrimp Creole

### 🌴

| 1 lb | Raw fresh shelled and deveined shrimp | 500 g |
|---|---|---|
| 1 tbsp | Fresh lime or lemon juice | 15 ml |
| 2 tbsp | Best quality vegetable oil | 30 ml |
| 2 tbsp | Butter | 30 ml |
| 1 | Large onion, sliced | 1 |
| ½ | Large green sweet pepper, chopped | ½ |
| 1 | Medium tomato, seeded and chopped | 1 |
| 2 | Garlic cloves, crushed | 2 |
| 2 tbsp | ❖ Busha Browne's Spicy Tomato Love-Apple Sauce | 30 ml |
| 1 tsp | ❖ Busha Browne's Spicy & Hot Pepper Sherry | 5 ml |

Put cleaned and prepared shrimps in a glass dish, squeeze lime juice over them and return to refrigerator until ready to be cooked.

Heat oil and fry crushed garlic until it is brown and the aroma rises. Discard garlic. Reduce heat. Add butter, onion and sweet pepper. Sauté lightly, then add drained shrimp and tomato and stir until shrimp turn pink, about 2-3 minutes. Add *Spicy Tomato Sauce* and *Pepper Sherry*, with salt and pepper to taste. Thicken if desired with 1 tsp (5 ml) cornstarch dissolved in cold water. Serve immediately on a bed of piping hot plain rice. Garnish as desired with parsley. Serves 4.

# Busha Browne's Curried Jonga

Jongas (or jangas) are wily fresh water crayfish. They hide under rocks in streams and only come out at night. They are rarely caught and are much prized by Jamaicans. Pieces of lobster or large shrimps may be substituted.

🌴 🌴 🌴

| | | |
|---|---|---|
| 2 | Medium onions, chopped | 2 |
| 3 | Garlic cloves, minced | 3 |
| 3 tbsp | Best quality vegetable or coconut oil | 40 ml |
| 2 tbsp | Best Indian curry powder | 30 ml |
| 1 tsp | Dry mustard | 5 ml |
| 2 lb | Raw, peeled crayfish | 1 kg |
| 1 tsp | ❖ Busha Browne's Spicy & Hot Pepper Sherry | 5 ml |
| 1 tbsp | ❖ Busha Browne's Original Spicy Planters Sauce | 15 ml |
| 1 tsp | ❖ Busha Browne's Pukka Hot Pepper Sauce | 5 ml |
| | Salt and black pepper to taste | |
| 1 | Large tomato, chopped | 1 |
| 2 tbsp | Butter | 30 ml |
| 2 tsp | Lime or lemon juice | 10 ml |
| 4 tbsp | ❖ Busha Browne's Original Banana Chutney | 60 ml |

Saute onions and garlic in oil until tender. Add curry powder and dry mustard, stirring for about 2 minutes. Add the crayfish, salt and black pepper with the three *Busha Browne's Sauces*. Add tomato. Cook uncovered until crayfish are firm and pink, about 15 minutes. Add butter and lime juice. Mix well. Serve on hot, steamed plain rice with *Banana Chutney* and other side dishes or 'sambals' (page 67). Serves 6.

# Caribbean Pumpkin & Shrimp

🌴

| | | |
|---|---|---|
| 1 | Small calabaza pumpkin | 1 |
| ½ lb | Cooked shrimps, picked and cleaned | 250 g |
| | Salt and pepper to taste | |
| 1 tbsp | ❖ Busha Browne's Original Spicy Planters Sauce | 15 ml |
| ½ cup | Busha Browne's Classic Béchamel Sauce (page 80) | 125 ml |

Cut pumpkin in halves and take out seeds and strings. Do not peel. Boil until cooked but not soft. Scoop out flesh leaving about ½ inch (1.25 cm) thick. Scallop edge of shells with sharp knife. Chop shrimps and mix with crushed pumpkin, seasonings, and *Busha Browne's Sauces*. Return to shells and bake in moderate oven for 20 minutes. Serves 4.

# Fowl–Young, Old & Game

"If God grants me the usual length of life, I hope to make France so prosperous that every peasant will have a chicken in his pot on Sunday."

–Henri IV of France, when he was crowned King in 1589.

# Chicken Victoria

Queen Victoria succeeded to Britain's throne in 1837, one year before the Emancipation Act came into force in 1838. She was beloved in Jamaica as "Missus Queen who set us free".

🌴

| | | |
|---|---|---|
| 4 lb | Chicken, cut into serving pieces | 2 kg |
| 1 tbsp | Lime or lemon juice | 15 ml |
| 1 tsp | Salt | 5 ml |
| ½ tsp | Freshly ground black pepper | 2 ml |
| 1 | Medium onion, sliced thinly | 1 |
| 1 | Clove garlic, crushed and chopped | 1 |
| 1 | Green sweet pepper, seeded and chopped | 1 |
| ½ tsp | ❖ Busha Browne's Pukka Hot Pepper Sauce | 2 ml |
| 1 tbsp | Best quality vegetable oil | 15 ml |
| 2 cups | Long grain rice | 500 ml |
| 1 cup | Mushrooms, sliced | 250 ml |
| ½ tsp | Annatto seeds, or saffron | 2 ml |
| 1 tbsp | ❖ Busha Browne's Spicy Tomato Love-Apple Sauce | 15 ml |
| 2-3 inch | Piece of lime peel | 5-8 cm |
| 1 tbsp | Lime juice | 15 ml |
| ¼ tsp | ❖ Busha Browne's Spicy & Hot Pepper Sherry | 1 ml |
| 4 cups | Concentrated chicken stock | 1 l |
| 3 tbsp | Gold Jamaican rum | 40 ml |

Squeeze fresh lime or lemon juice over the chicken pieces. Sprinkle well with salt and pepper. Add onions, garlic, green sweet pepper and the *Pukka Sauce* to chicken pieces. Cover and refrigerate for up to 24 hours. When ready to cook, shake seasoning off the chicken and reserve. Pat chicken pieces dry with paper towels.

Heat oil with annatto seeds in heavy bottomed casserole until oil becomes red and then discard the seeds. Sauté the chicken pieces until browned. Remove chicken pieces from casserole, and set aside.

To the oil in the saucepan, add the uncooked rice, the reserved seasoning, and sauté, stirring, until the oil is absorbed. Be careful that the rice does not burn. Return the chicken pieces to the saucepan and stir into rice. Add the mushrooms which have been lightly sautéed for about 5 minutes. If using saffron, add it at this point, along with the *Spicy Tomato Sauce*, the lime peel and lime juice, the *Pepper Sherry* and the chicken stock. Correct the seasoning. Cover and simmer gently until the rice is cooked and chicken is tender and the liquid has been absorbed, about ½ hour. Add the rum last and cook uncovered for about 5 minutes longer. A royal feast! Serves 6.

# Arroz con Pollo
## (Chicken & Rice)

🌴

| | | |
|---|---|---|
| 4 lb | Chicken, cut into serving pieces | 2 kg |
| 2 | Cloves garlic | 2 |
| ½ tsp | Oregano | 2 ml |
| 2 tsp | Salt | 10 ml |
| ¼ tsp | Freshly ground black pepper | 2 ml |
| 2 tbsp | Lime or lemon juice | 30 ml |
| 1 tbsp | ❖ Busha Browne's Original Spicy Planters Sauce | 15 ml |
| 4 tbsp | Olive oil | 60 ml |
| 1 | Onion, chopped | 1 |
| ½ cup each | Green sweet pepper and tomato, chopped | each 125 ml |
| 1 | Bay leaf | 1 |
| 4 oz | Ham, chopped coarsely (optional) | 125 g |
| 1 tbsp | Fresh cilantro or parsley chopped | 15 ml |
| 3 cups | Concentratd chicken stock | 750 ml |
| 2 cups | Long grain rice | 500 ml |
| 1 tbsp | Capers | 15 ml |
| 2 oz | Pitted green olives, sliced | 60 g |
| 3 tbsp | ❖ Busha Browne's Spicy & Hot Pepper Sherry | 40 ml |
| ½ cup | Snow peas | 125 ml |
| 2 | Sweet red peppers, sliced | 2 |

Mix together the garlic, oregano, salt, pepper and lime or lemon juice and rub into the chicken pieces with the *Planters Sauce*. Let them stand to marinate for about an hour.

Heat the oil in a heavy, deep covered saucepan and sauté the drained chicken pieces until golden. Remove the chicken pieces from saucepan and set aside temporarily. Sauté the onion and green pepper in the remaining oil. Return the chicken pieces to the saucepan. Add any remaining marinade with the tomatoes, bay leaf, ham (if used), cilantro and 2 cups (500 ml) of chicken stock. Cover and simmer for ½ hour. At the end of this time, drain and measure the liquid in the pan and make up to 4 cups (1 litre) by adding chicken stock or boiling water. Return to pan, add the rice, the capers, olives, chicken pieces and other seasonings. Cover and cook over low heat until the liquid has been absorbed and the rice is tender, about 30 minutes.

Sprinkle the *Pepper Sherry* on the hot rice, and stir in the snow peas and red sweet pepper strips thoroughly. Return to heat just long enough to heat through. Serves 6.

# Planter's Fricasséed Chicken

🌴

| | | |
|---|---|---|
| 5 lb | Chicken pieces | 2.5 kg |
| 1 tbsp | Lime or lemon juice | 15 ml |
| | Salt and freshly ground black pepper to taste | |
| 2 tbsp | ❖ Busha Browne's Original Spicy Planters Sauce | 30 ml |
| ¼ tsp | ❖ Busha Browne's Pukka Hot Pepper Sauce | 1 ml |
| 2 | Cloves garlic, crushed in a press | 2 |
| 3 | Stalks escallions, chopped | 3 |
| 2 tsp | Cornstarch, dissolved in cold water | 10 ml |
| 1 tbsp | Dried thyme | 15 ml |
| 2 | Small tomatoes, seeded and chopped | 2 |
| 2 cups | Concentrated chicken stock | 500 ml |
| ¼ cup | Oil for frying | 60 ml |
| 2 | Onions, sliced | 2 |

Wash chicken pieces. Rub down with lime or lemon juice. Sprinkle with salt and pepper. Rub with *Busha Browne's Sauces*, garlic, thyme, escallion, onions and put in bowl. Add tomatoes and set aside for 1 hour.

Heat oil in large deep skillet until very hot. Brown the chicken pieces quickly on both sides and place in bowl with juices from marinade. Drain oil and chicken fat from skillet, retaining only 1 tbsp (15 ml). Return chicken pieces to skillet, cover and simmer 25 minutes or until chicken is tender. Thicken as desired by mixing cornstarch and cold water to which a spoonful of hot gravy is added before all is returned to the gravy. Correct seasoning and serve piping hot. Serves 6.

# Hall's Delight Curried Chicken

🌴 🌴

| | | |
|---|---|---|
| *Use the same ingredients as for Planters Fricasséed Chicken adding* | | |
| 5 tbsp | Best Indian Curry Powder | 70 ml |
| 2 cups | Coconut milk (page 20) | 500 ml |

Wash chicken and rub in and out with lime juice. Cut into small pieces and brown in hot oil in a heavy-bottomed casserole. Set aside in a bowl.

To the oil remaining in the casserole, add, in order, onions, escallion and garlic followed by curry powder: stir, and add tomatoes, sauces and coconut milk. Stir until thickened. Add chicken stock slowly while stirring until thoroughly blended. Add browned chicken: bring to the boil, then lower heat, cover and simmer for about 1 hour. Serves 6.

# Busha's Stoshus Chicken

"Stoshus" is a Jamaican patois expression meaning smart, stylish, well-dressed, or high-class.

🌴

| | | |
|---|---|---|
| 2 x 3 lb | Fresh whole young chickens | 2 x 1.5 kg |
| ¼ tsp | Onion powder | 1ml |
| ¼ tsp | Garlic powder | 1ml |
| ¼ tsp | Ground pimento berries (allspice) | 1ml |
| ¼ tsp | Black pepper | 1ml |
| 1 tsp | Salt | 5 ml |
| ¼ tsp | ❖ Busha Browne's Pukka Hot Pepper Sauce | 1ml |
| 1 tbsp | ❖ Busha Browne's Original Spicy Planters Sauce | 15 ml |
| 2 tbsp | Soy sauce | 30 ml |

Put all the dry spices in a small dish, and mix to a paste with the soy sauce and the two *Busha Browne's Sauces*. Rub thoroughly into chickens, inside and out. Cover and refrigerate for about 1 hour. Roast in 350° F (180°C) oven, basting occasionally to brown, for about 1½ hours or until juices run clear. Cover with foil and leave in warm, unlit oven until ready to serve. For readymade gravy: deglaze the roasting pan. Serves 6.

TIP: *Freeze gravy overnight. Fat can be easily removed. The defatted gravy is excellent on crushed boiled green bananas, crushed pumpkin, potatoes or rice.*

# Hunt's Bay Chicken Paprika

🌴 🌴

| | | |
|---|---|---|
| 3 lb | Fresh young chicken, cut in pieces | 1.5 kg |
| ¼ cup | Unsalted butter | 60 ml |
| 1 | Medium onion, chopped | 1 |
| 1 tbsp | Paprika | 15 ml |
| ½ tsp | ❖ Busha Browne's Pukka Hot Pepper Sauce | 2 ml |
| 1 cup | Red Stripe Beer | 250 ml |
| 2 tbsp | Green sweet pepper, finely minced | 30 ml |
| | Salt and pepper to taste | |
| 1 cup | Sour cream or plain unsweetened yogurt | 250 ml |

In a deep covered casserole, sauté the onion in the butter. Add paprika, *Pukka Sauce* and the chicken pieces. Brown chicken on all sides. Add beer and green pepper. Cover and simmer for about 45 minutes until chicken is tender. Pour off liquid and strain into separate saucepan. Add sour cream (or yogurt), heat (do not allow to boil) and add chicken pieces. Serve piping hot with plain steamed rice. Serves 4.

# Westmoreland White Wing Feast

Westmoreland, considered the Wilderness Parish, is a haven
for hunters during the all-too-short bird-shooting season. For
centuries Jamaicans have vied for the best way to prepare a
traditional 'bird-feed' of white-wing, baldpate, wild duck and
other Jamaican game birds.

| | | |
|---|---|---|
| 12 | Game Birds | 12 |
| 4 tbsp | Lime juice | 60 ml |
| 2 tsp | Salt | 10 ml |
| 1 tsp | Ground pimento (allspice) | 5 ml |
| 4 | Cloves garlic, crushed in a press | 4 |
| 3 | Large onions | 3 |
| 6 | Stalks escallion | 6 |
| 12 | Seasoning (cherry) tomatoes | 12 |
| 1 tsp | Fresh thyme leaves | 5 ml |
| 1 tbsp | ❖ Busha Browne's Spicy & Hot Pepper Sherry | 15 ml |
| 1 tbsp | ❖ Busha Browne's Original Spicy Planters Sauce | 15 ml |
| ½ tsp | ❖ Busha Browne's Pukka Hot Pepper Sauce | 2 ml |
| ¼ cup | Best quality vegetable oil | 60 ml |
| 2 tbsp | Butter | 30 ml |
| | GRAVY | |
| 1 cup | Concentrated chicken stock | 250 ml |
| ¼ cup | Dry red wine | 60 ml |
| 1 tbsp | ❖ Busha Browne's Spicy & Hot Pepper Sherry | 15 ml |

Allow 3 cleaned and plucked birds per person. Set aside the giblets to be
cooked separately. Squeeze lime juice over the birds and wash well inside
and out. Allow to drain. Make a paste with the dried seasonings and the
*Busha Browne's Sauces* and rub well into the birds. Place in a glass or
earthenware container and sprinkle with the chopped tomato, onion and
escallion. Refrigerate and allow seasoning to soak in for 12-24 hours.

Cook giblets in 2 cups (500 ml) unsalted water and dice finely. Reserve
stock. Make stuffing (page 61) and refrigerate.

Brown birds in a skillet in a mixture of oil and butter, and cook down
in their own juices for about 1 hour. Remove the birds and reserve the
stock. Allow the birds to cool enough to handle, then stuff loosely. Place
stuffed birds in a roasting pan and immediately finish them for 30–45
minutes in a 350°F (180°C) oven. Serve with gravy. Serves 4.

GRAVY: Deglaze the pot in which the birds were cooked. Add the leftover
stock from the giblets, chicken stock, red wine and and *Pepper Sherry*. Add
giblets. Thicken as desired by mixing cornstarch with water to which a
spoonful of hot gravy is added before all is returned to the gravy. Correct
the seasoning and serve hot.

# Busha's Game Bird Stuffing
## (for 12 Small Birds)

🌴

| | | |
|---|---|---|
| 2 tbsp | Best quality vegetable oil | 30 ml |
| 2 tbsp | Butter | 30 ml |
| 2 tbsp | Diced onion | 30 ml |
| ¼ cup | Chopped sweet green pepper | 60 ml |
| ¼ cup | Chopped celery | 60 ml |
| 4 | Seasoning (cherry) tomatoes | 4 |
| ½ cup | Water chestnuts, finely diced | 125 ml |
| 2 tbsp | Chopped parsley | 30 ml |
| ½ tsp | Salt | 2 ml |
| ¼ tsp | Black pepper | 1 ml |
| ½ tsp | Dried sage | 2 ml |
| ¼ tsp | Freshly grated nutmeg | 1 ml |
| 1 | Clove garlic, crushed in a press | 1 |
| 1 tbsp | ❖ Busha Browne's Hot & Spicy Pepper Sherry | 15 ml |
| 1 tbsp | ❖ Busha Browne's Original Spicy Planters Sauce | 15 ml |
| ¼ tsp | ❖ Busha Browne's Pukka Hot Pepper Sauce | 1 ml |
| 2 cups | Dried breadcrumbs | 500 ml |
| 1 cup | Stock made from bird giblets | 250 ml |

Make stock with giblets and trimmings from birds (see page 60). Set aside.

Fry onions, sweet pepper, tomatoes, garlic and other vegetables in a mixture of oil and butter. Butter gives a good flavour and the oil prevents the butter from burning. Add dried seasonings, water chestnuts and the three *Busha Browne's Sauces*. Add the stock and then stir in the breadcrumbs, mixing to make a light dressing. Add more stock if required.

Allow to cool, and use immediately to stuff birds loosely. Any leftover stuffing can be baked in a ramekin and served as a side dish with some of the game bird gravy. Excellent with either of the *Pepper Jellies*.

## Stuffing for Wild Duck

🌴

Wild duck can be prepared as for game birds adding 1 tsp (5 ml) *grated orange zest* with the seasonings and *orange juice* for half the chicken stock.

Stuffing is also as for game birds but breadcrumbs may be replaced with cooked crushed sweet potato or half breadcrumbs and half wild rice.

Tip: *The finished birds can be glazed with ¼ cup (60 ml) each melted Busha Browne's Ginger Pepper Jelly and Busha Browne's Burned Orange Marmalade. Brush on with pastry brush. Garnish with orange slices.*

# Busha Browne's Pineapple Chicken

❦

| | | |
|---|---|---|
| 3 lb | Broiler/fryer chicken, cut into serving pieces | 1.5 kg |
| 1 tbsp | Lime or lemon juice | 15 ml |
| 1 | Onion, finely chopped | 1 |
| 2 | Garlic cloves, crushed and chopped | 2 |
| 3 tbsp | Best quality vegetable oil | 40 ml |
| 1 | Small fresh pineapple, chopped | 1 |
| ¾ cup | Water chestnuts, sliced | 180 g |
| ½ tsp | ❖ Busha Browne's Pukka Hot Pepper Sauce | 2 ml |
| 1 tbsp | ❖ Busha Browne's Original Spicy Planters Sauce | 15 ml |
| 3 | Medium tomatoes, peeled, seeded and chopped | 3 |
| | Salt and freshly ground black pepper to taste | |
| 1 cup | Snow peas | 250 ml |
| 1 tbsp | Chopped chives or spring onions | 15 ml |

Season chicken pieces. Squeeze fresh lime or lemon juice over and rub in salt and pepper, onion and garlic. Leave to marinate for at least ½ hour, or for up to 24 hours, refrigerated. Heat the oil in a heavy saucepan, and sauté the chicken pieces until golden on both sides. Add the onion and garlic and cook until onion is tender. Add the pineapple and any juice, water chestnuts, *Pukka Sauce*, *Planters Sauce* and tomatoes. Correct the seasoning. Cover and simmer until the chicken is tender, about 45 minutes. Add a little concentrated chicken stock if necessary. During the last 10 minutes, add the snow peas and chives. Delicious with *Busha Browne's Chutneys*. Serves 6.

# Planter's Chicken Liver Kebabs

❦

| | | |
|---|---|---|
| 2 lb | Fresh chicken livers | 1 kg |
| ¼ cup | ❖ Busha Browne's Spicy & Hot Pepper Sherry | 50 ml |
| 12 | Miniature onions (or cut pieces) | 12 |
| 3 | Green sweet peppers, cut in pieces | 3 |
| | Salt and pepper to taste | |

Marinate chicken livers in *Pepper Sherry* overnight in refrigerator. Sauté onions and chicken livers briefly in butter to partially cook until livers are firm enough to be skewered. Thread chicken livers on long skewers alternating with onions, tomatos and green peppers. Finish under the grill. Delicious with either of the *Chutneys*. Serves 6.

# The Meat
# of the Matter

"For its merit, I will Knight it
And call it Sir-Loin."

–Charles II of England

# Pukka Planter's Beef Stew
🌴 🌴

| | | |
|---|---|---|
| 3 lb | Lean beef, cubed | 1.5 kg |
| 1 tsp | Salt | 5 ml |
| ½ tsp | Black pepper | 2 ml |
| ¼ tsp | Garlic powder | 2 ml |
| 2 | Sprigs of fresh thyme | 2 |
| 2 tbsp | ❖ Busha Browne's Original Spicy Planters Sauce | 30 ml |
| ½ tsp | ❖ Busha Browne's Pukka Hot Pepper Sauce | 2 ml |
| 1 | Large onion, sliced | 1 |
| ½ | Sweet pepper, julienne | ½ |
| 3 | Plum tomatoes | 3 |
| 3 | Stalks of escallion, chopped | 3 |
| ¼ cup | Best quality vegetable oil | 60 ml |
| 3 | Carrots, sliced | 3 |
| ½ | Cho-cho | ½ |
| 4 large | Irish potatoes, cut in halves | 4 |
| ½ cup | Dry red wine | 125 ml |

If possible, use meat that has not been frozen. Put into glass dish, sprinkle with powdered dry spices. Add *Planters Sauce* and *Pukka Sauce* and mix thoroughly. Add onion, sweet pepper, escallion and tomatoes and mix again, lightly. Cover and leave to "soak" in refrigerator for at least 1 hour.

Heat the oil in a deep saucepan. Brown the pieces of meat, a few at a time. When all are sealed, return to the saucepan with the vegetables, cover and lower heat to a simmer, and allow to cook for about 1 hour. It will not be necessary to add liquid if the temperature is kept low, so it is important to just simmer this. About 20 minutes before the meat is ready, add the potatoes, and the ½ cup (125 ml) of dry red wine if desired. This dish is better after refrigerating for a day. Serves 6.

# Country Roast Beef
🌴

Rub a roast of beef with *Busha Browne's Original Spicy Planters Sauce*, salt, pepper and garlic powder. Leave covered overnight in refrigerator. To sear, place in hot 500°F (250°C) oven, and immediately reduce heat to 350°F (180°C). Roast without basting until cooked to one's taste. Gravy can be made from pan drippings. Juice will have remained in roast.

TIP: *In order to prevent juices running out of the roast into the roasting pan, do not pierce the roast in any way or insert any garlic or spices.*

# Busha's Spicy Beef Tongue

Tender spiced tongue is a delicacy in Jamaica.

🌴 🌴

| | | |
|---|---|---|
| 3 lb | Lean baby beef tongue (smoked optional) | 1.5 kg |
| 1½ cups | Red Stripe Beer | 375 ml |
| 1½ cups | Concentrated chicken stock | 375 ml |
| 10 | Pimento berries (allspice) | 10 |
| 10 | Whole black peppercorns | 10 |
| 6 | Whole cloves | 6 |
| 2 tsp | Salt | 10 ml |
| 2 | Bay leaves | 2 |
| 1 tbsp | ❖ Busha Browne's Original Spicy Planters Sauce | 15 ml |
| ½ tsp | ❖ Busha Browne's Pukka Hot Pepper Sauce | 2 ml |
| 2 tbsp | Herb vinegar | 30 ml |

Tie tongue in circle with stout string and place in saucepan with beer and chicken stock. Bring to boil. Reduce heat, cover and simmer for 1 hour. Add seasonings, *Busha Browne's Sauces* and vinegar. Cover and simmer until tender, about 2 hours. Allow to cool in broth.

Remove string and skin from tongue, and force into round earthenware bowl. Pour broth over tongue and cover with plate and place a stone or other weight to press the tongue into the shape of the bowl. Refrigerate at least 24 hours. Unmold tongue with gelatine onto plate. Slice across tongue to maintain circular shape or cut into diagonal slices. Spoon gelatine onto each serving. Superlative with *Busha Browne's Chutneys* or *Pepper Jellies*. Serves 6.

# Glazed Ham with Pepper Jelly

🌴

| | | |
|---|---|---|
| 1 | Baked ham with bone | 1 |
| | Whole cloves to cover surface of ham | |
| ¼ cup | Prepared Dijon mustard | 60 ml |
| 3 cups | Pineapple juice | 750 ml |
| ½ cup | ❖ Busha Browne's Original Pepper Jelly | 125 ml |

Rub skinned, scored ham with prepared Dijon mustard and spread with the *Pepper Jelly*. Dot with cloves. Place ham in roasting pan and add pineapple juice. Bake in oven preheated to 350° F (180° C) for an hour basting frequently. Skim fat from pan juices and pour juices into a sauceboat. Accompany ham with mustard, additional *Pepper Jelly*, or *Busha Browne's Chutneys* and pan juices.

# Busha Browne's Special Roast Pork
## 🌴 🌴

| | | |
|---|---|---|
| 4 lb | Lean pork leg or loin roast, rolled and tied | 2 kg |
| | MARINADE | |
| 1 cup | Orange juice | 250 ml |
| 1 cup | ❖ Busha Browne's Lime Pepper Jelly | 250 ml |
| ¼ cup | ❖ Busha Browne's Spicy & Hot Pepper Sherry | 60 ml |
| | GLAZE | |
| ¾ cup | ❖ Busha Browne's Lime Pepper Jelly | 180 ml |
| ¼ cup | ❖ Busha Browne's Spicy & Hot Pepper Sherry | 60 ml |

Place pork in glass dish or large plastic bag. Warm marinade ingredients together until jelly is melted, then pour over pork. Cover tightly or seal in plastic bag. Leave to "soak" in refrigerator for 12 to 24 hours. Heat oven to 450°F (230° C), remove pork from marinade, and put on rack in oven. Reduce heat immediately to 350°F (180°C) and roast joint for 1½ hours, basting occasionally with marinade.

Combine glaze ingredients, and brush on to roast for the last 10-15 minutes of cooking. If you are using a meat thermometer the temperature should read 160° F (80°C). If not, insert a two-pronged kitchen fork or carving fork into the roast. If the juices run clear, the roast should be done. Let rest 10 to 15 minutes before removing string and carving. Serves 6. TIP: *This roast can also be cooked over a covered grill or barbecue. Busha Browne's Ginger Pepper Jelly is excellent with roast pork.*

# Barbecued Spare Ribs
## 🌴 🌴

| | | |
|---|---|---|
| 4 lb | Lean young pork spare ribs | 2 kg |
| 1 tbsp | Lime or lemon juice | 15 ml |
| | Salt and pepper to taste | |
| | BARBECUE SAUCE | |
| ¼ cup | Honey | 60 ml |
| ½ cup | ❖ Busha Browne's Original Spicy Planters Sauce | 125 ml |
| ½ cup | ❖ Busha Browne's Spicy Tomato Love-apple Sauce | 125 ml |
| 1 tbsp | ❖ Busha Browne's Spicy & Hot Pepper Sherry | 15 ml |

Cut spare ribs into sections of two or three ribs each. Sprinkle ribs with lime juice, salt and pepper. Cover with foil and grill until nearly cooked. Remove foil. To make the SAUCE, combine honey with the three *Busha Browne's Sauces*, and brush on to the chops for the last 5 minutes. Serves 4. (The same recipe can be used for tender lean pork chops.)

# Cabarita Curried Mutton
## ("Curry Goat")

The East Indians, who from 1845 were brought as indentured labourers to Jamaica, introduced curried dishes to the island. Traditionally, the bones are chopped and left in the stew for added flavour.

🌴 🌴 🌴

| | | |
|---|---|---|
| 3 lb | Lean, boneless cubed mutton | 1.5 kg |
| 4 cloves | Garlic, crushed in a press | 4 cloves |
| 1 large | Onion, diced | 1 large |
| 3 | Stalks escallion, chopped | 3 |
| 1 tsp | Salt | 5 ml |
| ½ tsp | Freshly ground black pepper | 2 ml |
| 3 tbsp | Best quality Indian curry powder | 40 ml |
| 1 tsp | Dry mustard | 5 ml |
| 1 tsp | Onion powder | 5 ml |
| 1 tsp | Freshly grated ginger | 5 ml |
| 2 sprigs | Fresh thyme | 2 sprigs |
| 2 tbsp | Fresh lime juice | 30 ml |
| 1 tbsp | ❖ Busha Browne's Original Spicy PlantersSauce | 15 ml |
| 1 tsp | ❖ Busha Browne's Pukka Hot Pepper Sauce | 5 ml |
| 3 | Medium Irish potatoes, cubed | 3 |
| 3 | Carrots, chunked | 3 |
| 1 tbsp | Best quality vegetable oil | 15 ml |
| 1 cup | Coconut milk (page 20) | 250 ml |

Mix dried seasonings in a glass bowl with the *Busha Browne's Sauces*. Add cubed mutton and mix thoroughly with spices and herbs. Then add the fresh onion, escallion and lime juice, along with the cubed potatoes. Refrigerate covered for 24 hours or overnight.

The following day, heat the oil in a heavy saucepan and add seasoned mutton. Stir to brown lightly for 5-10 minutes. Add thyme sprigs. Do not add liquid, but cover tightly and reduce heat to a simmer. Allow to cook gently, stirring occasionally for about 45 minutes, adding liquid only if necessary. At the end of 45 minutes add the cup of coconut milk. Cook for 10 minutes more. Serve over steamed white rice with *Busha Browne's Spicy Fruit Chutney* and a selection of the following side dishes or "Sambals":

*Freshly grated coconut*  *Fancy plumped raisins*
*Sliced ripe bananas*  *Diced unpeeled cucumber*
*Minced sweet onion*  *Roti or pita pocket bread*
*Chopped hard-boiled egg*  *Chopped unsalted peanuts*
*Tomato & sweet pepper salsa*

# Walkerswood Oxtail & Beans

In Jamaica, oxtail is considered a special treat.

🌴 🌴

| | | |
|---|---|---|
| 3 lb | Lean oxtail, jointed | 1.5 kg |
| 2 tbsp | Best quality cooking oil | 30 ml |
| 5 cups | Beef stock | 1.25 l |
| 4 | Plum tomatoes | 4 |
| 3 | Medium onions, chopped | 3 |
| | Clove of garlic, finely minced | |
| 2 tbsp | ❖ Busha Browne's Original Spicy Planters Sauce | 30 ml |
| ½ tsp | ❖ Busha Browne's Pukka Hot Pepper Sauce | 2 ml |
| | Salt and freshly ground black pepper to taste | |
| 2 cups | Cooked broad beans or lima beans | 500 ml |

Brown the prepared oxtail pieces in hot oil in a deep heavy-bottomed saucepan. Add beef stock, tomato, onions, garlic and *Busha Browne's Sauces*. Simmer until oxtail is tender and liquid has been reduced by half. Add salt and pepper, correct seasoning and add beans last. Serves 6.

# Stuffed Cho-cho or Zucchini

🌴

| | | |
|---|---|---|
| 2 | Cho-chos or zucchini squash | 2 |
| ½ lb | Ground beef or lamb | 250 g |
| 1 | Chopped onion | 1 |
| | Salt and pepper to taste | |
| 1 tsp | ❖ Busha Browne's Original Spicy Planters Sauce | 5 ml |
| 1 tbsp | ❖ Busha Browne's Spicy Tomato Love-Apple Sauce | 15 ml |
| ½ cup | Dried breadcrumbs | 125 ml |
| 1 tbsp | Dried grated cheese, preferably Cheddar | 15 ml |

Cut cho-chos or zucchini in half lengthwise, and steam until tender but not overdone. Carefully scoop out the flesh, leaving about ¼ inch (.5 cm) on the skin to form four cases. While the vegetable is cooking, sauté the ground beef with the onion, *Busha Browne's Sauces* and other seasonings. Then add the cooked pulp from the cho-cho and season to taste. Pack lightly into the vegetable cases, cover with breadcrumbs which have been mixed with the grated cheese, and place a pat of butter on each case. Bake in a hot oven until golden brown and heated through. Serves 4.

TIP: *If cooked rice or pasta is available, this can be added to the meat mixture. Sweet peppers or eggplants (aubergine) also make excellent vegetable cases.*

# Jamaican Jerk Barbecue

There was a young man from New York
Whose craving was wine with Jerk pork
He set up his spit,
With Pimento leaves lit
Then siphoned his wine through a cork

*–Jamaican Limerick*

# *Notes on Jerk —*
## *the unique Jamaican Barbecue*

As far back as 1698, a French priest named Père Labat wrote a description of a picnic which he organized in the island of Martinique, after the style of the 'boucaniers'. His description of building the grill or 'boucan' and the seasoning of the whole pig tallies precisely with the methods used today at the roadside 'jerk pits' still to be seen in Jamaica.

> "To make the Boucan four forked sticks, about four feet long and as thick as your arm, are driven into the ground to form an oblong structure about four feet long by three feet wide. Crosspieces of wood are placed in the forks of these posts. On these, one arranges the grill, which is also made of sticks, and all this contraption is well tied together with lianes. The pig is placed on this bed on its back, the belly wide open and kept in position with sticks to prevent it from closing up when the fire is lighted …The belly of the pig must be filled with lime-juice and plenty of salt and crushed pimento…A large couii (calabash or gourd) full of gravy and another full of lime-juice, pepper, salt and pimento stand in the centre of the table and from these, each guest mixes his gravy according to his taste…"
>
> —From: *The Memoirs of Père Labat, 1693-1705.*

> "We had at dinner a land tortoise and a barbecued pig, two of the best and richest dishes that I ever tasted, the latter in particular, which was dressed in the the true Maroon fashion, being placed on a barbecue (a frame of wickerwork, through whose interstices the steam can ascend) filled with peppers and spices of the highest flavour, wrappt in plantain leaves and then buried in a hole filled with hot stones by whose vapour it is baked, no particle of juice being thus suffered to evaporate. I have eaten several other good Jamaica dishes, but none so excellent as this…"
>
> —From: *Journal of a West India Proprietor* by Matthew Lewis, 1834.

# Jamaican Jerk Pork

"Our dinner, at 6, was really so profuse, that it is worth describing. The first course was entirely of fish, excepting jerked hog, in the centre, which is the way of dressing it by the Maroons..." From *Lady Nugent's Journal, March 1802.*

🌴 🌴 🌴

| | | |
|---|---|---|
| 2 lb | Pork leg or loin | 1 kg |
| 2 tbsp | ❖ Busha Browne's Jerk Seasoning | 10 ml |
| 1 tsp | ❖ Busha Browne's Pukka Hot Pepper Sauce | 5 ml |
| 1 inch | Fresh Jamaican ginger-root, grated | 2.5 cm |
| 3 | Garlic cloves, minced | 3 |
| ½ tsp | Salt | 2 ml |
| 2 tbsp | Best quality cooking oil | 30 ml |

Combine the *Jerk Seasoning* and *Pukka Sauce* with grated ginger-root, minced garlic, salt and oil. Rub into pork. Marinate overnight in refrigerator. Prepare and light grill or barbecue 3 to 4 hours before meal at which pork is to be served. Allow coals to burn down until coated with grey ash. Remove pork from refrigerator, reserve the marinade, and place pork on greased grill, or on a spit over the fire. Cook slowly, turning and basting every 10 minutes until juices run clear. Remember that pork should be cooked until well done. Time will vary according to thickness of joint. If cooking suckling pig, time will be reduced. Skin should be crisp. To serve: cut jerk pork into bite size pieces. Serves 6.

TIP: *In Jamaica the wood and leaves of the Pimento (Allspice) tree are used to barbecue jerked meats. Pimento gives an incomparable aroma and flavour.*

# Busha Browne's Jerk Pork Roast

🌴

| | | |
|---|---|---|
| 2 lb | Pork roast | 1 kg |
| 3 | Garlic cloves, sliced | 3 |
| 2 tsp | ❖ Busha Browne's Jerk Seasoning | 10 ml |
| 1 inch | Fresh Jamaican ginger root, grated | 2.5 cm |
| ½ tsp | Salt | 2 ml |
| 1 | Onion chopped finely | 1 |
| 2 tbsp | ❖ Busha Browne's Original Pepper Jelly | 10 ml |

Combine all the above ingredients, and rub well into pork. Allow to soak for 2-3 hours. Roast at 325° F (165° C) for approximately 2 hours, or until juices run clear, and internal temperature, if you are using a thermometer, reads 180° F (80° C). Garnish, carve and serve. Serves 6.

# Jamaican Jerk Chicken

🌴 🌴 🌴

| 4 lb | Roasting chicken | 2 kg |
|---|---|---|
| 1 tbsp | Lime or lemon juice | 15 ml |
| 1 tbsp | ❖ Busha Browne's Jerk Seasoning | 15 ml |

Rub whole chicken with lime or sprinkle with lemon juice. Spread the *Jerk Seasoning* over whole chicken. Rub in well, and allow to marinate for at least 2 hours. Roast in oven at 325°F (160°C) for 1½ to 2 hours. Baste continually with pan drippings. Do not overcook. Carve on platter, and serve with seasoned rice, fried plantain and green salad. Serves 8.

TIP: *To grill: Use above-mentioned seasoning in proportion to chicken parts, and marinate in refrigerator for 2 hours. If a less pungent flavour is required, use ½ tablespoon (8 ml) Jerk Seasoning.*

VARIATION: *Whole fish may be prepared in the same way. Pineapple, mango or other 'soothing' fruit complements the hot jerk flavour with either chicken or fish.*

# Jerk Chicken Salad

🌴 🌴

| 4 | Boneless chicken breasts | 4 |
|---|---|---|
| 2 tbsp | ❖ Busha Browne's Jerk Seasoning | 30 ml |
| ¼ cup | Olive oil | 60 ml |
| 4 | Medium onions, julienne | 4 |
| 1 | Sweet red pepper, cut in strips | 1 |
| 1 cup | Bean sprouts | 250 ml |
| 1 | Sweet green pepper, cut in strips | 1 |
| ¼ cup | Extra virgin olive oil | 60 ml |
| ¼ cup | Parsley, chopped | 60 ml |
| 3 | Black olives, slivered (optional) | 3 |
| ¼ cup | Great House Vinaigrette Dressing (page 30) | 60 ml |

Mix together the *Jerk Seasoning* and olive oil and brush on trimmed chicken breasts. Allow to marinate covered and refrigerated, for about an hour, or longer if possible. Then lay the chicken breasts, each of which has been separated into two pieces, flat in roasting pan; cover with foil and bake in pre-heated oven for 10 minutes at 325° F (160° C) or until done. Cool, then cut into bite-size strips. Refrigerate.

Sauté onions, peppers and bean sprouts in batches in remaining olive oil, cool and mix with chicken, parsley and black olives. Refrigerate.

When all ingredients have been cooled, pour dressing over all and toss lightly but thoroughly. Serve with tomato and salad greens. Serves 4.

# Jamaican Jerk Yellowtail Snapper

🌴

| | | |
|---|---|---|
| 2 lb | Fresh Yellowtail Snapper fish fillet or Swordfish steaks | 1 kg |
| ¼ cup | Extra virgin olive oil | 60 ml |
| 2 tbsp | ❖ Busha Browne's Jerk Seasoning | 30 ml |
| | or | |
| | ❖ Busha Browne's Spicy Jerk Sauce. | |

### SALSA

| | | |
|---|---|---|
| 5 tbsp | ❖ Busha Browne's Spicy Tomato Love-Apple Sauce | 75 ml |
| 2 cups | Peeled, seeded tomatoes, coarsely chopped | 500 ml |
| ½ cup | Red or purple onion, coarsely chopped | 125 ml |
| 2 tbsp | Cilantro, or parsley, coarsely chopped | 30 ml |
| 2 | Cloves garlic, minced | 2 |
| 1 tsp | Lime or lemon juice | 5 ml |

FISH: Brush fillets with a thin coat of oil and rub each with *Jerk Seasoning* or *Spicy Jerk Sauce*. Place on fish rack and grill over hot coals or broil in very hot oven 550°F (280°C), for about 4 minutes on each side.
SALSA: Combine all ingredients in blender or food processor. Blend briefly just long enough to give a coarsely chopped look. Refrigerate.
TO SERVE: Arrange fish attractively on plates. Spoon the salsa alongside each piece of fish. Serve with boiled parsley potatoes. Serves 4.

# Devilled Shrimp & Mango Kebabs

🌴

| | | |
|---|---|---|
| 3 lb | Large shrimp, shelled and deveined | 1.5 kg |
| ¼ cup | Best quality vegetable oil | 60 ml |
| 1 tbsp | Grated fresh Jamaican ginger root | 15 ml |
| 2 tbsp | ❖ Busha Browne's Jerk Seasoning | 30 ml |
| 2 | Firm ripe mangoes cut into 1 in (2.5 cm) cubes | 2 |

Combine oil, ginger and *Jerk Seasoning* in a bowl. Add the shrimp and marinate for 4-6 hours, turning occasionally.
    Arrange the shrimp and mangoes on each skewer alternating shrimp and mango pieces. Grill for 5-8 minutes, turning and basting until cooked. These can also be sautéed in butter with 1 tsp (5 ml) melted *Busha Browne's Original Pepper Jelly* and then arranged on skewers. Serves 6-8.
TIP: *Jerk Seasoning* and *Spicy Jerk Sauce* may be used equally well with beef, chicken, fish or pork.
VARIATION: *Firm ripe peaches may be used if mangoes are not available.*

# Busha Browne's Reggae Wings

🌴

| | | |
|---|---|---|
| 3 lb | Chicken wings | 1.5 kg |
| ¼ cup | Best quality vegetable oil | 60 ml |
| 1 | Small onion, chopped | 1 |
| 1 | Fresh large lime or lemon, juiced | 1 |
| 2 tbsp | Soy sauce | 30 ml |
| ¼ cup | ❖ Busha Browne's Spicy Jerk Sauce | 60 ml |
| 2 tbsp | Escallions, finely chopped | 30 ml |

Place wings in a bowl. Blend all ingredients and pour over wings. Marinate for 24-48 hours in the refrigerator. Grill the wings, basting with marinade for 20 minutes, cooking slowly and evenly until juices run clear. Serve piping hot with either of *Busha Browne's Chutneys*. Serves 4-6.

# Busha's Jerk Pork Chops

🌴

| | | |
|---|---|---|
| 4 | Pork chops | 4 |
| 2 tsp | ❖ Busha Browne's Jerk Seasoning | 10 ml |
| 1 tsp | Lime juice (optional) | 5 ml |

Rub *Jerk Seasoning* and lime juice over chops. Prepare grill or barbecue and grill chops until juices run clear. Serves 2.

# Busha's Spicy Lobster Tails

🌴 🌴

| | | |
|---|---|---|
| 4 | Medium lobster tails | 4 |
| ¼ cup | Lime or lemon juice | 60 ml |
| 2 tsp | ❖ Busha Browne's Jerk Seasoning | 30 ml |
| ½ tsp | ❖ Busha Browne's Pukka Hot Pepper Sauce | 2 ml |
| | Freshly grated nutmeg | |

Melt butter in skillet: add lime or lemon juice and *Jerk Seasoning* and *Pukka Sauce*. Sauté lobster tails lightly in butter mixture. Sprinkle with freshly grated nutmeg and garnish with parsley sprig and slices of lime and serve immediately with *Busha Browne's Lime Pepper Jelly*.
VARIATION: *The addition of Busha Browne's Spicy Tomato Love-Apple Sauce and grated cheese gives this dish an interesting new character.*

# Accompaniments & Embellishments

"May your rice never burn."

–Traditional Chinese New Year's greeting

# Jamaican Coat of Arms
## (Rice & Peas)

Before refrigeration was available, fresh meat was expensive and difficult to obtain. The Sunday pot of Rice and Peas would be prepared, using a bit of salt beef or a salted pig's tail, which then would be cut up and a piece would be placed on top of each portion of the Rice and Peas as "The Watchman".

🌴 🌴

| | | |
|---|---|---|
| 1 cup | Red peas (kidney beans) | 250 ml |
| 1 cup | Coconut milk (page 20) | 250 ml |
| 8 cups | Water | 2 l |
| 2 | Rashers bacon, or salted pig's tail (optional) | 2 |
| 1 | Sprig thyme | 1 |
| 1 in | Piece fresh ginger root | 2.5 cm |
| ½ tsp | ❖ Busha Browne's Pukka Hot Pepper Sauce | 2 ml |
| 1 tbsp | ❖ Busha Browne's Original Spicy Planters Sauce | 15 ml |
| 2 | Cloves garlic, crushed | 2 |
| 3 | Stalks escallion or chives, chopped | 3 |
| 2 cups | Long grain rice | 500 ml |
| 1 tsp | Salt (optional if required) | 5 ml |

Put peas to soak for at least 2 hours, or overnight if they are old. Then put them on to boil with the bacon or pig's tail. Prepare the coconut milk, and add to the boiling peas. Cook until the peas are tender.

Bruise the ginger root and add with the thyme and *Pukka Sauce* together with the garlic, *Planters Sauce* and escallion. Add salt only if necessary as the meat should provide enough. Simmer for a few moments to blend the flavours. Remove from heat until cool enough to handle. Strain off the liquid in the pot, and measure it. If necessary, add water to make the liquid amount to 4 cups (1 litre) or twice the amount of rice.

Return the liquid to the pot with the peas and bring back to boiling. (Some cooks recommend that the water should be about 1 inch (2.5 cm) or "two fingers" above the level of the rice.)

Wash the rice and add to the boiling liquid. Cover the pot as soon as it returns to the boil. Simmer for approximately 20 minutes over very low heat. The rice is ready as soon as the liquid disappears, but the rice should still be grainy. This recipe makes 8 generous servings.

VARIATION: *Fresh green gungo peas (pigeon peas) may be used instead of dried red kidney beans. This is traditionally served during the holiday season.*

NOTE: *Although beans and rice are enjoyed in various combinations throughout the Caribbean and even Central America, this version of Rice and Peas is considered one of the national dishes of Jamaica. The combination of pulse and grain makes for a nutritionally complete meal.*

# Busha's Seasoned Rice

🌴

| | | |
|---|---|---|
| 2 tbsp | Best quality vegetable oil | 30 ml |
| 2 tbsp | Butter | 30 ml |
| 1 | Large onion, finely chopped | 1 |
| 2 | Stalks escallions, finely chopped | 2 |
| ¼ cup | Sweet green pepper, finely chopped | 60 ml |
| | Salt to taste | |
| ½ cup | ❖ Busha Browne's Spicy Tomato Love-Apple Sauce | 125 ml |
| ½ cup | Best quality tomato juice | 125 ml |
| 1 cup | Water | 250 ml |
| 1 cup | Long grain rice | 250 ml |

Sauté chopped vegetables in oil and butter. Add *Spicy Tomato Sauce*, tomato juice, salt and water, and bring to a boil. Add rice, stir and bring to the boil reduce heat and steam for 20 minutes. Turn off heat and allow to stand for a few minutes. Fluff with a fork before serving.

# Turned Cornmeal Creole

🌴

| | | |
|---|---|---|
| ¼ cup | Best quality vegetable oil | 60 ml |
| 1 | Large tomato, finely diced | 1 |
| 1 | Large sweet green pepper, finely diced | 1 |
| 1 doz | Tender young okras | 12 |
| 1 | Large onion, finely diced | 1 |
| ¼ cup | Escallion, finely diced | 60 ml |
| | Salt and black pepper to taste | |
| ½ tsp | Garlic powder | 2 ml |
| 1 tbsp | ❖ Busha Browne's Original Spicy Planters Sauce | 15 ml |
| 1 qt | Water | 1 l |
| 2 cups | Stone ground yellow cornmeal | 500 ml |

Heat oil, and sauté chopped vegetables gently. Add salt, pepper and garlic powder and *Planters Sauce*. Add all the water and bring to the boil. Add all the cornmeal at once and stir vigorously with a whisk for about 10 minutes. When the mixture is smooth, cover, reduce the heat and allow to steam for about 30 minutes or until thoroughly cooked. Turn into a greased round pudding basin or small indiviual bowls to mould, and then turn out onto a plate. Garnish and serve, cut into wedges. Serves 6.

# Hellshire Beach Festival

This savoury-sweet fried dumpling is named for the celebration held on the first weekend in August, the anniversary of Jamaica's independence in 1962. Festival is always served with fried fish, but is also a fine treat at teatime.

🌴

| | | |
|---|---|---|
| 1 cup | Stone ground yellow cornmeal | 250 ml |
| ¾ cup | All purpose flour | 180 ml |
| ¼ cup | Light brown sugar | 60 ml |
| 1 tsp | Baking powder | 5 ml |
| ½ tsp | Salt | 2 ml |
| 1 | Whole egg | 1 |
| 1 tsp | ❖ Busha Browne's Original Spicy Planters Sauce | 5 ml |
| 1 cup | Water | 250 ml |

Mix cornmeal and flour, add sugar and salt. Beat egg lightly and add water combined with *Planters Sauce* and mix. Add egg mixture to cornmeal mixture and mix together to form a dough. Tear off pieces of dough and roll into oval shapes and deep fry. Serve with fried fish.

# Busha's Favourite Boiled Dumplings

These are rather solid dumplings, but are much beloved by all Jamaicans, especially children and the men who work on construction crews, or who walk, sometimes for miles to work in the fields, planting or reaping crops. They generally carry a used, clean five gallon oil pan with them in which they boil their dumplings, yam and other 'ground provisions'.

🌴

| | | |
|---|---|---|
| 1 cup | All-purpose flour | 250 ml |
| 1 tsp | Salt | 5 ml |
| ½ tsp | Baking powder (optional) | 2 ml |
| ½ tsp | ❖ Busha Browne's Original Spicy Planters Sauce | 2 ml |
| ¼ cup | Water | 60 ml |

Put flour into a small bowl. Add salt and baking powder if required and stir. Make a hole in the middle and add water mixed with *Planters Sauce* all at once. Mix with a wooden spoon until mixture forms a dough. Dust your hands with flour and knead the dough lightly. Tear off bits of dough and roll between your hands into long 'spinners' or else form round balls which are then flattened for 'dumplings'. Drop into boiling soup and cook for about 15 minutes or until they rise to the surface, when they should be done. Use in soups or stews. Serves 6.

VARIATION: *To make cornmeal dumplings, use ½ cup (125 ml) of flour, mixed with ½ cup (125 ml) of cornmeal.*

# Jamaican Duckanoo
## (Blue Drawers)

This is a development of a traditional West African spicy-sweet pudding, which was originally made with plantains or other starchy foods such as green banana, cassava flour and later cornmeal. Sometimes called 'tie-leaf' as it is divided into little parcels wrapped in banana leaves, which are then boiled or steamed. A bluish stain is left on the pudding by the banana leaves when cooked, thus the name 'blue-drawers'.

| | | |
|---|---|---|
| 1 cup | Stone ground yellow cornmeal | 250 ml |
| ½ cup | All purpose flour | 125 ml |
| 2 cups | Coconut milk (page 20) | 500 ml |
| ½ cup | Dark brown sugar | 250 ml |
| ½ cup | Raisins | 125 ml |
| ½ cup | ❖ Busha Browne's Original Pepper Jelly | 125 ml |

Mix cornmeal and flour with coconut milk. Add sugar, raisins and *Pepper Jelly*. Spoon into squares of banana leaves which have been wilted by dipping into boiling water to make them pliable. Tie into parcels with string. If banana leaves are unavailable, use squares of foil. Place in boiling water and steam for 45 minutes. Serves 4.

# Busha Browne's Savoury Pastry

| | | |
|---|---|---|
| 2 cups | All purpose flour | 500 ml |
| 1 tsp | Salt | 5 ml |
| ⅔ cup | Shortening, chilled | 160 ml |
| 1 tsp | ❖ Busha Browne's Original Spicy Planters Sauce | 5 ml |
| 5 tbsp | Cold water | 70 ml |

Sift flour, measure, add salt and sift again. 'Cut in' half of the shortening thoroughly, until mixture resembles coarse cornmeal. Cut in remaining shortening coarsely, or until particles are about the size of peas. Sprinkle water combined with *Planters Sauce*, 1 tbsp (15 ml) at a time over small portions of the mixture and gather together the flour particles as they absorb the water. Use only sufficient water to hold the pastry together. Press all together lightly. Wrap dough in waxed paper and chill for at least an hour. Roll out to size required. Will make sufficient pastry for 9" (23cm) doublecrust pie. (Dough may be divided and wrapped separately.)
TIP: *A food processor produces flaky short pastry.*
VARIATION: *For* DESSERT PASTRY, *substitute 1 tsp (5 ml) melted Busha Browne's Twice-Boiled Guava Jelly for the Planters Sauce.*

# Busha Browne's
# Classic Béchamel Sauce

❦

| | | |
|---|---|---|
| 3 tbsp | Butter (for best flavour) | 40 ml |
| 3 tbsp | All purpose flour | 40 ml |
| 1 tsp | Dry mustard | 5 ml |
| ½ tsp | Salt | 2 ml |
| ¼ tsp | Freshly ground black pepper | 1 ml |
| ¼ tsp | Freshly powdered mace | 1 ml |
| 1 tbsp | ❖ Busha Browne's Original Spicy Planters Sauce | 15 ml |
| 1 cup | Evaporated milk, scalded | 250 ml |

In a heavy saucepan over direct heat, or in the top of a double boiler, over hot water, melt the butter and stir in the flour. Allow to cook for a few minutes, then add the mustard, salt, black pepper and powdered mace. Stir to blend. Slowly add the hot milk combined with the tablespoon *Planters Sauce*, stirring all the time. This sauce is delicious with all cooked or steamed vegetables.

VARIATION: *For* BUSHA BROWNE'S *SPICY* CHEESE SAUCE, *slowly add ½ cup grated Cheddar Cheese, heat, but do not allow to boil and stir until thick.*

## Busha's Hollandaise Sauce

| | | |
|---|---|---|
| 3 | Egg yolks | 3 |
| 2 tbsp | Wine vinegar | 30 ml |
| ½ tsp | ❖ Busha Browne's Spicy & Hot Pepper Sherry | 2 ml |
| ½ cup | Unsalted butter | 125 ml |
| ¼ tsp | Salt | 1 ml |
| | Freshly ground black pepper | |

Place the egg yolks, vinegar and the *Pepper Sherry* in the top of a double saucepan and stir together until they are thoroughly combined. Place over hot, not boiling water, and heat gently, stirring continuously until the yolks are thickened. Add the butter, piece by piece, whisking over gentle heat until all the butter has been added and has melted. Beat sauce until it is thick. Remove from the heat and stir in the salt and pepper. Keep warm over hot (not boiling) water for a short time and then serve warm over eggs or vegetables.

TIP: *It is important to keep this sauce warm, not boiling, or it will curdle. If this happens, combine 1 tsp (5 ml) of lemon juice with 1 tbsp (15 ml) of curdled sauce in a bowl, and whisk vigourously until thickened. Continue to add the curdled sauce spoonful by spoonful, whisking between additions until sauce thickens.*

# Busha Browne's Jiffy Mayonnaise

🌴

| 2 | Small eggs | 2 |
|---|---|---|
| 1 tsp | Powdered mustard | 5 ml |
| 1 tsp | Salt | 5 ml |
| ¼ tsp | ❖ Busha Browne's Pukka Hot Pepper Sauce | 1 ml |
| 2 tsp | Granulated sugar | 5 ml |
| 1¼ cups | Extra virgin olive oil, divided | 300 ml |
| ¼ cup | Lime juice | 60 ml |

Put first five ingredients into blender with ¼ cup (50 ml) of the olive oil. Cover and blend until thoroughly mixed. While the blender is still running, slowly add a further ½ cup (250 ml) of the olive oil. When that has been absorbed, gradually add the lime juice, processing until thoroughly blended. Add the remaining ½ cup (250 ml) olive oil slowly, blending until the mixture has thickened. Stop and stir occasionally, scraping down the sides of the blender jar. Refrigerate and use within 2 or 3 days.

# Green Island Mayonnaise

🌴

| 1¼ cup | Busha Browne's Jiffy Mayonnaise | 300 ml |
|---|---|---|
| 2 tbsp | Parsley, finely chopped | 30 ml |
| 2 tbsp | Fresh dillweed or fennel, finely chopped | 30 ml |
| 2 tbsp | Fresh chives, finely chopped | 30 ml |
| 2 tbsp | Fresh watercress, finely chopped | 30 ml |
| ¼ cup | Steamed callaloo, finely chopped | 60 ml |
| 1 tsp | ❖ Busha Browne's Spicy & Hot Pepper Sherry | 5 ml |

Combine all in blender. Serve with cold fish, shellfish or vegetables.

# Bombay Curry Mayonnaise

🌴

| 1 cup | Busha Browne's Jiffy Mayonnaise | 250 ml |
|---|---|---|
| 1 tbsp | ❖ Busha Browne's Ginger Pepper Jelly | 15 ml |
| 1 tsp | Best Indian curry powder | 5 ml |
| 1 tbsp | ❖ Busha Browne's Spicy Fruit Chutney | 15 ml |

Combine all ingredients in blender. Serve with fruit, fish or chicken salads.

# Busha Browne's Variations on Salsa
## Fresh Tomato-Cucumber Salsa

❦

| | | |
|---|:---:|---:|
| 1 | Medium tomato | 1 |
| 1 | Cucumber | 1 |
| 1 | Small onion | 1 |
| 1 tbsp | Spiced cane vinegar | 15 ml |
| 1 tsp | ❖ Busha Browne's Hot & Spicy Pepper Sherry | 5 ml |
| ¼ tsp | Salt | 1 ml |
| ¼ tsp | Garlic powder | 1 ml |

Chop tomato and cucumber. Slice onion thinly and separate into rings. Mix all together lightly and sprinkle with vinegar and *Pepper Sherry*, salt and garlic powder. This salsa is best served with curried meats or as a tasty picante side salad. May be used as a "Sambal" (page 67).

## Banana Salsa

❦ ❦

| | | |
|---|:---:|---:|
| 1 | Large ripe, firm banana, peeled and diced | 1 |
| ½ | Large red or green sweet pepper, seeded and diced | ½ |
| 2 tbsp | Fresh mint or cilantro, finely chopped | 30 ml |
| 1 | Stalk escallion or chives, finely chopped | 1 |
| 2 tbsp | Fresh lime juice | 30 ml |
| 2 tbsp | ❖ Busha Browne's Original Banana Chutney | 30 ml |
| 1 tbsp | Fresh peeled ginger, minced | 15 ml |
| 2 tbsp | Olive oil | 30 ml |
| 1 tsp | ❖ Busha Browne's Pukka Hot Pepper Sauce | 5 ml |
| | Salt and freshly ground black pepper to taste | |

Combine all ingredients in a bowl, tossing lightly to combine. Adjust seasonings. Delicious on grilled seafood, or with chips as an appetizer.

## Orange-Pineapple Salsa

Melt 1 cup (250 ml) *Busha Browne's Burned Orange Marmalade* with water. Add ½ cup (125 ml) fresh chopped pineapple and 2 tbsp (30 ml) rum. Simmer for a few minutes. Cool and blend the sauce to a smooth consistency. Dissolve 2 tbsp (30 ml) cornstarch in water, add to sauce, then return to the saucepan, and heat, stirring until the sauce thickens. This salsa is sweet and is superb served with grilled chicken or fish.

# Indulgences

"Sweets for the sweet."

–William Shakespeare

# Busha Browne's Classic Crêpes with Orange Sauce

| | | |
|---|---|---|
| 2 | Whole eggs | 2 |
| 1 cup | Milk | 250 ml |
| 1 cup | All purpose flour | 250 ml |
| ½ tsp | Salt | 2 ml |
| ¼ tsp | Ground cinnamon | 1 ml |
| ½ cup | ❖ Busha Browne's Burned Orange Marmalade | 125 ml |
| | Vegetable oil to cook crêpes | |
| | Granulated sugar | |
| | Lemon or lime slices to garnish | |
| | SAUCE | |
| ½ cup | ❖ Busha Browne's Burned Orange Marmalade | 125 ml |
| ½ cup | Boiling water | 125 ml |
| ¼ cup | Brandy or aged Jamaican gold rum | 60 ml |
| 1 tbsp | Cornstarch | 15 ml |
| 2 tbsp | Cold water | 10 ml |

Sieve flour and salt into a mixing bowl. In another bowl, whip eggs, milk and cinnamon together. Make a hole in the flour, pour in the eggs and milk. Mix with a wooden spoon until smooth. Cover and put aside for at least half an hour until bubbles rise to the surface.

When ready to cook, heat a small frying pan until a drop of water dances on the surface. Put a spoonful of oil in the pan, and then add about ¼ cup (60 ml) of batter. Tilt the pan until the batter spreads thinly. When the mixture is set, flip the crêpe over and cook for a few seconds. Stack the crêpes on a plate with waxed paper between them and keep warm until each one has been cooked.

Spread each crêpe with a tablespoon(15 ml) of Marmalade, and roll. Place in an ovenproof casserole, sprinkle with sugar and keep warm until ready to serve. Garnish with sliced lime or lemon, and granulated sugar and serve with Orange Sauce (below). Makes about 8 crêpes.

SAUCE: Melt Marmalade in boiling water in a saucepan. Dissolve cornstarch in cold water and add to hot mixture. Heat to thicken, add brandy or rum and serve over crêpes. One teaspoon (5 ml) of butter may be added.

# Busha's Orange-Banana Split

In an oval dish, place two scoops of grape-nut or vanilla ice cream. Split a ripe banana in half lengthwise and cut into quarters, arranging them around the ice-cream. Top with a tablespoon (15 ml) of Busha Browne's Burned Orange Marmalade and finely chopped cashews or peanuts.

# Llanrumney Bananas Flambé

The property Llanrumney in St Mary was once owned by Captain Henry Morgan, the notorious pirate, who mended his ways and became Lieutenant Governor of Jamaica in 1674.

| 4-6 | Firm ripe bananas | 4-6 |
|---|---|---|
| ¼ cup | Icing sugar or confectioner's sugar | 60 ml |
| 1 tbsp | Butter | 15 ml |
| 4 tbsp | ❖ Busha Browne's Burned Orange Marmalade | 60 ml |
| 1 tsp | Fresh lime or lemon juice | 5 ml |
| 1 tsp | Water, or as needed | 5 ml |
| 1 tbsp | Aged Jamaican gold rum | 15 ml |
| | Ice cream for topping | |

Peel bananas and take off all strings. Slice in half and then lengthwise about ¼ in (.7 cm) thick. Roll in confectioner's sugar. Heat butter in frying pan, and sauté sugar covered pieces of banana a few at a time. When all are done, return them to frying pan, together with the *Marmalade*, lime juice and water. Stir to melt the marmalade, adding another teaspoonful hot water if needed. Be careful not to bruise bananas.

Just before serving, heat the tablespoonful of rum in a large metal spoon, preferably silver, until it bursts into flame. Pour over the bananas, and carry into a darkened room. Delicious served with vanilla ice cream.

# Busha's Banana Fritters

| 3 | Ripe bananas, peeled | 3 |
|---|---|---|
| 1 | Whole egg | 1 |
| 1 tbsp | Granulated sugar | 15 ml |
| 1 tsp | Lime juice | 5 ml |
| 3 tbsp | All purpose flour | 40 ml |
| ½ tsp | Baking powder | 2 ml |
| 2 tbsp | Vegetable oil for frying | 30 ml |

Sieve together flour and baking powder. Mash bananas quickly until smooth and add lime juice. Beat egg and sugar together, add bananas and then flour mixture. Pour oil in frying pan: fry fritters by spoonfuls. Serve with Marmalade Sauce (page 84).

# Busha Browne's Banana Sundae

Place a scoop of vanilla ice cream in a pretty serving bowl and top with a tablespoon of *Busha Browne's Original Banana Chutney*. Amazing!

# Scones & Guava Jelly

These scones have always been popular for Jamaican afternoon tea served any time from 4 pm to 5 pm. They are very similar to the 'biscuits' that are made in the American South.

| | | |
|---|---|---|
| 4 cups | All-purpose flour (1 lb) | 500 g |
| ½ tsp | Salt | 2 ml |
| ½ cup | Shortening | 125 ml |
| 6 tsp | Double acting baking powder | 30 ml |
| 1 cup | Warmed milk | 250 ml |

Put flour, salt and baking powder into food processor. Cut shortening into small lumps and add. Pulse until mixture looks like cornmeal crumbs. Add warm milk and pulse until mixture comes together into a ball. Flour hands and take out of food processor bowl, and place on floured sheet of wax paper. Pat out into rectangle about ½ in (1.3 cm) thick. Cut into 2 in (5 cm) rounds. Place on greased cookie sheet and brush with milk and bake in hot oven 400° F (200° C) for about 10 minutes.

Split and butter. Spread with *Busha Browne's Twice-Boiled Guava Jelly*.

# Queen of Puddings

A traditional Jamaican sweet. The term 'Queen' generally indicates that lime or lemon is the principal flavouring.

| | | |
|---|---|---|
| 4 slices | Day old bread | 4 slices |
| 4 tbsp | Granulated sugar | 60 ml |
| 1 cup | Milk | 250 ml |
| ¼ cup | Butter | 60 ml |
| 2 | Eggs, separated | 2 |
| 1 tsp | Grated rind of a lime or lemon | 5 ml |
| 2 tbsp | ❖ Busha Browne's Twice-boiled Guava Jelly | 30 ml |
| 2 tbsp | Confectioner's sugar | 30 ml |

Butter an ovenproof casserole. Tear the slices of stale bread into approximately 1 in (2.5 cm) squares. Place in the casserole; sprinkle the granulated sugar over and mix lightly. Heat together the milk and butter and pour over the bread and sugar. Leave to soak for 30 minutes. Separate eggs and stir the yolks into the bread and milk, together with the lime or lemon rind. Bake in 350°F (180° C) oven for about 40 minutes or until set.

Remove from oven, and spread with *Guava Jelly*. To make meringue, beat egg whites until stiff, add 2 tbsp (30 ml) of confectioner's sugar and beat until peaks hold. Spread by spoonfuls over bread and milk mixture and bake in very hot 450° F (230° C) oven until meringue is set and tips are brown. Serve at room temperature. Serves 4.

# Guava Gizzadas

These small coconut tarts, probably of Spanish-Jewish origin have been a favourite with with generations of Jamaican children and grown-ups alike.

| | | |
|---|---|---|
| | *Busha Browne's Dessert Pastry (page 79)* | |
| 1 | *Mature dry coconut, skinned and grated* | 1 |
| | *or* | |
| 1 cup | *Grated unsweetened coconut* | *250 ml* |
| 2/3 cup | *Dark brown sugar* | *160 ml* |
| 1 tsp | *Freshly grated ginger root* | *5 ml* |
| 1/2 tsp | *Freshly grated nutmeg* | *2 ml* |
| 1/2 cup | *Water* | *125 ml* |
| | ❖ *Busha Browne's Twice-Boiled Guava Jelly* | |

Prepare pastry and line tartlet pan or shallow muffin pans. Put sugar and water, grated coconut, grated ginger root and nutmeg to boil until it all comes together. Fill pastry cases and bake at 350 F° (180°C) until golden brown but still moist. While still hot top each gizzada tartlet with a generous teaspoonful of *Guava Jelly*. Serve at room temperature.

Fresh coconut gives the best flavour and a moist texture.

# Busha's Bread Pudding

| | | |
|---|---|---|
| 5 - 6 | *Slices stale bread* | 5 - 6 |
| 2 tbsp | *Butter* | *30 ml* |
| 2 cups | *Milk* | *500 ml* |
| 1 cup | *Light brown sugar* | *250 ml* |
| 1 tsp | *Vanilla* | *5 ml* |
| 1/4 tsp | *Freshly grated nutmeg* | *1 ml* |
| 1/4 cup | *Plumped raisins* | *60 ml* |
| 2 | *Whole eggs, beaten* | 2 |
| | ❖ *Busha Browne's Twice-Boiled Guava Jelly* | |
| | ❖ *Busha Browne's Burned Orange Marmalade* | |

Butter the slices of bread, then dice and place in buttered casserole. Mix milk, sugar, vanilla and nutmeg and pour over the bread. Add raisins which have been rinsed and cleaned. Put aside for 30 minutes. Add the beaten eggs and stir well. Pour into an ovenproof casserole, and place in preheated 350° F (180° C) oven for approximately 45 minutes or until top is brown. Serve with topping of either *Guava Jelly* or *Marmalade*.

# Busha Browne's
# Jamaican Plum Pudding
## (Christmas Pudding)

This fruit pudding or cake is a development of an Old English Plum Pudding with the addition of Jamaican rum. Family recipes are handed down from generation to generation. In the holiday season, puddings are shipped from Jamaica to absent family members all over the world. The same recipe, baked instead of steamed, is also used for wedding cakes.

| | | |
|---|---|---|
| 2 cups | Butter (1 lb) | 500 ml |
| 2 cups | Dark brown sugar | 500 ml |
| 1 dozen | Eggs | 1 dozen |
| 3 cups | All purpose flour | 750 ml |
| 1 tsp | Double acting baking powder | 5 ml |
| 2 cups | Dried breadcrumbs | 500 ml |
| 1 tsp | Salt | 5 ml |
| 2 tbsp | Mixed spice | 30 ml |
| 1 tbsp | Cinnamon | 15 ml |
| 1 tsp | Freshly grated nutmeg | 5 ml |
| 2 tsp | Vanilla | 10 ml |
| ½ cup | ❖ Busha Browne's Burned Orange Marmalade | 125 ml |
| ½ cup | ❖ Busha Browne's Twice-Boiled Guava Jelly | 125 ml |
| 1 gal | Rum-soaked dried fruit (page 89) | 4 l |

This mixture will make two large puddings. Prepare pans with tight lids by lining with greased and floured parchment paper.

Sieve flour with breadcrumbs, spices and leavening. Cream butter and sugar, then add eggs and beat well. Add sieved flour mixture. Add vanilla and *Marmalade* and *Guava Jelly*. Fold in the soaked fruit until wooden spoon stands upright in batter.

Divide the batter between the tins, cover and seal them. If the pans do not have covers, place a double thickness of parchment paper over the tops, and tie this down tightly with string. Put the covered pans in a slow oven 300° F (150°C). On the bottom shelf put a large roasting pan full of boiling water to keep the oven moist. Bake for about 4 hours, replenishing the boiling water on the bottom shelf as needed, until pick put into centre of the puddings comes out clean. The covered pans can also be steamed in a pressure cooker, or in boiling water on top of the stove.

Serve with Brandy Sauce or Rum Butter. The puddings will keep for several months, well-wrapped in a dry cool place, and will darken with age. VARIATION: *The same mixture is also traditionally baked (instead of steamed) and is used for Jamaican wedding cakes. The cake is covered with a layer of marzipan (almond paste) and tastefully decorated with Royal Icing.*

# Rum Soaked Dried Fruit
## (for Jamaican Plum Pudding)

For at least a month before making the puddings, put the following dried fruit to soak in rum or any other liquor except port wine. In Jamaica, bottles of "soak fruit" are ready for baking in many kitchens all the year round.

| | | |
|---|---|---|
| 2 lb | Dried prunes | 1 kg |
| 1 lb | Dark brown sugar | 500 g |
| 2 lb | Raisins | 1 kg |
| 1 lb | Currants | 500 g |
| ½ lb | Crystallized citron peel, chopped coarsely | 250 g |
| ½ lb | Dates, pitted and chopped | 250 g |
| ½ lb | Chrystalised red cherries, cut in quarters | 250 g |
| 2 qt | Aged Jamaican gold rum | 2 l |

Stew the prunes with the sugar, cool and then remove the stones. Chop coarsely. Clean, wash and dry the raisins and currants, and chop coarsely. Combine all the fruit in a large, covered wide-mouthed bottle, or other container that can be sealed of about 1 gallon (4 litres) capacity. Pour the rum over all, making sure that the fruit is completely covered. Cover tightly. Leave to soak for at least 4 weeks or for up to 1 year.

# Guava Rum Butter

| | | |
|---|---|---|
| 1 cup | Butter (½ lb) | 250 ml |
| 2 cups | Confectioners sugar | 250 ml |
| ¼ cup | Aged Jamaican gold rum or brandy | 60 ml |
| ¼ tsp | Cinnamon | 1 ml |
| ¼ cup | ❖ Busha Browne's Twice-Boiled Guava Jelly | 60 ml |

Cream butter then add icing sugar, cinnamon, Jamaican rum or brandy and Guava Jelly. For Hard Sauce, refrigerate until set. For soft sauce, heat over warm water, stirring continuously, then pour over pudding slices when serving. Add a little water if too thick.

# Orange Brandy Sauce

Melt ¼ cup (60 ml) butter. Add ¼ cup (60 ml) flour. Add slowly 1½ cups (375 ml) boiling water and ¼ cup (60 ml) dark brown sugar. Bring to boil, lower heat and cook for 15 minutes, stirring. Add ¼ cup (60 ml) Busha Browne's Burned Orange Marmalade melted in ¼ cup (60 ml) good brandy. Sprinkle in ¼ tsp (1 ml) freshly grated nutmeg. Serve hot.

# Busha's Sweet Potato Pone

| 2 lb | Yellow sweet potatoes | 1 kg |
|---|---|---|
| 1½ cups | Yellow cornmeal | 375 ml |
| 6 cups | Coconut milk (see page 20) | 1.5 l |
| 2½ cups | Dark brown sugar | 625 ml |
| 1 tsp | Cinnamon | 5 ml |
| ½ tsp | Ground pimento berries (allspice) | 2 ml |
| 1½ tsp | Grated nutmeg | 7 ml |
| 1½ tsp | Salt | 7 ml |
| 1 tsp | Double acting baking powder | 5 ml |
| 1 tsp | Vanilla | 5 ml |
| ½ cup | ❖ Busha Browne's Burned Orange Marmalade | 125 ml |
| ¼ cup | Plumped raisins | 60 ml |
| 2 tbsp | Butter | 30 ml |

Grate raw peeled sweet potatoes in a large bowl. In a separate bowl mix together all dry ingredients except the brown sugar.

In another bowl, mix together sugar, coconut milk, *Marmalade* and vanilla. Add all dry ingredients, including grated sweet potato. Stir to eliminate lumps. (Mixture should be runny, not thick). Pour into greased rectangular glass baking dish and bake in moderately hot oven 350° F (180° C) for about 1 hour or until pudding is set. Sprinkle on raisins (some will sink to the bottom) and dot with butter. Bake the pone for another half to three-quarters of an hour.

This recipe makes a soft gooey pone to be eaten warm, spooning over self-made sauce. Refrigerated, it becomes solid and can be cut with a knife.

# Lime Cay Pudding

| 1 tbsp | Butter | 15 ml |
|---|---|---|
| 1 cup | Granulated sugar | 250 ml |
| 2 tbsp | All purpose flour | 30 ml |
| 2 tsp | Freshly squeezed lime juice | 10 ml |
| ¼ tsp | Grated lime rind | 2 ml |
| 2 | Eggs, separated | 2 |
| 1 cup | Fresh milk | 250 ml |

Cream butter and sugar. Add flour, lime juice and rind. Beat egg yolks and whites separately. Add egg yolks to butter mixture, followed by milk. Quickly fold in stiffly beaten egg whites. Bake in glass pudding dish set in water in a moderate oven preheated to 350°F (180°C) for about an hour. Serve hot, spooning over the sauce found in the bottom of the baking dish. VARIATION: *The same recipe may be made with orange juice and rind.*

# Liberal Libations

The horse and mule live thirty years
And nothing know of wine and beers.
The goat and sheep at thirty die.
And never taste of Scotch and Rye.
The cow drinks water by the ton,
And at eighteen is nearly done.
The dog at fifteen cashes in
Without the aid of Rum or Gin.
The cat in milk and water soaks,
And then in twelve short years it croaks.
The modest, sober, bone-dry hen
Lays eggs for nogs, then dies at ten.
All animals are strictly dry.
They sinless live and swiftly die.
But simple, Ginful, Rum-soaked men
Survive for three score years and ten.
*And some of us, the mighty few*
*Stay pickled till we're ninety-two!*

– Anonymous

# Busha Browne's Perfect Bloody Mary

🌴 🌴

| | | |
|---|---|---|
| 6 oz | Best quality tomato juice | 180 ml |
| 3 oz | Vodka | 90 ml |
| 2 tsp | ❖ Busha Browne's Spicy & Hot Pepper Sherry | 10 ml |
| 4 drops | ❖ Busha Browne's Pukka Hot Pepper Sauce (optional) | 4 drops |
| | A pinch of celery salt | |
| 2 tsp | Lime or lemon juice | 10 ml |

Fill two chilled heavy-bottomed 6 oz glasses three-quarters full with crushed ice. Pour over tomato juice, vodka, *Busha Browne's sauces* and lime or lemon juice in that order. Stir vigorously and garnish with celery stalk and sprinkling of dried paw paw seeds, or freshly ground black pepper. VARIATION: *The substitution of clam juice for half of the tomato juice makes this drink a "CAESAR", much enjoyed by Canadians.*

# Busha Browne's Perfect Bullshot

🌴

| | | |
|---|---|---|
| 3 oz | Chicken or beef consommé | 90 ml |
| 1¹/₂ oz | Vodka | 40 ml |
| 1 tsp | ❖ Busha Browne's Spicy & Hot Pepper Sherry | 5 ml |
| 1 tsp | Lime or lemon juice | 5 ml |

Shake or stir well with ice. Serve in 6 oz glass garnished with slice of lime.

# Busha's Perfect Bloody Bull

🌴 🌴 🌴

| | | |
|---|---|---|
| 3 oz | Best quality tomato juice | 90 ml |
| 3 oz | Beef consommé | 90 ml |
| 3 oz | Vodka | 90 ml |
| 1 tsp | ❖ Busha Browne's Spicy & Hot Pepper Sherry | 5 ml |
| 2 drops | ❖ Busha Browne's Pukka Hot Pepper Sauce (optional) | 2 drops |
| 1 tsp | ❖ Busha Browne's Original Spicy Planters Sauce | 5 ml |
| 1 tsp | Lime or lemon juice | 5 ml |

Pour first three ingredients over ice in a chilled 10 oz (300 ml) heavy-bottomed glass. Add the three *Busha Browne's Sauces* and stir. Garnish with a young celery stalk with some of its leaves.

# Busha Browne's Spicy Dry Martini

| | | |
|---|---|---|
| 1 tsp | Extra dry vermouth | 5 ml |
| 2 oz | Dry gin | 60 ml |
| 1/2 tsp | ❖ Busha Browne's Spicy & Hot Pepper Sherry | 2 ml |

In a chilled, heavy-bottomed 4 oz (125 ml) glass, place 2 cubes of ice. Pour over the vermouth, gin and the *Pepper Sherry*. Stir quickly and add an olive or a cocktail onion as preferred.

# Sligo Gin Sling

| | | |
|---|---|---|
| 1 1/2 oz | Dry gin | 40 ml |
| 1 tbsp | Freshly squeezed lime juice | 15 ml |
| 1 tbsp | ❖ Busha Browne's Twice Boiled Guava Jelly | 15 ml |
| | Carbonated water | |

Melt *Guava Jelly* in a little boiling water to make guava syrup. Mix together ingredients including guava syrup and pour over ice cubes in a tall, chilled glass. Add carbonated water and garnish with a slice of lime.

# Planter's Gimlet

| | | |
|---|---|---|
| 7 1/2 oz | Dry gin | 225 ml |
| 4 oz | Freshly squeezed orange juice | 125 ml |
| 1 tbsp | Busha Browne's Twice Boiled Guava Jelly | 15 ml |
| 1 tbsp | Freshly squeezed lime juice | 15 ml |

Melt *Guava Jelly* in a little boiling water to make guava syrup. Pour all ingredients over crushed ice in two tall glasses, stir and garnish with slices of orange twist.
VARIATION: *Vodka may be used instead of gin as well lime juice to replace orange juice in either case.*

# Busha's Maiden's Prayer

| | | |
|---|---|---|
| 1 oz | Dry gin | 30 ml |
| 1 oz | Cointreau or Triple Sec | 30 ml |
| 1 oz | Freshly squeezed lime juice | 30 ml |
| Dash | ❖ Busha Browne's Spicy & Hot Pepper Sherry | Dash |

Pour ingredients over ice and stir well. Strain and pour into chilled stemmed cocktail glass. Garnish with a cherry on a toothpick.

# Great House Margarita

| | | |
|---|---|---|
| 1¹/₂ oz | Jamaican white rum | 40 ml |
| 1¹/₂ tbsp | Freshly squeezed lime juice | 20 ml |
| ¹/₂ tsp | ❖ Busha Browne's Spicy & Hot Pepper Sherry | 2 ml |
| 1 oz | Wild orange liqueur | 30 ml |
| ¹/₂ cup | Crushed ice | 125 ml |

Rub rim of stemmed glass with orange rind and dip in coarse salt. In blender, liquefy rum, lime juice, *Pepper Sherry*, orange liqueur and crushed ice for a few seconds. Pour into prepared glass which has been chilled.

# Busha's Banana Daiquiri

| | | |
|---|---|---|
| 1¹/₂ oz | Aged Jamaican gold rum | 40 ml |
| 1¹/₂ oz | Freshly squeezed lime juice | 40 ml |
| 1 tsp | Confectioner's sugar | 5 ml |
| 1 tsp | ❖ Busha Browne's Spicy & Hot Pepper Sherry | 5 ml |
| ¹/₂ oz | Wild orange liqueur | 15 ml |
| 1 | Medium sized banana, sliced | 1 |

Combine all ingredients with a cup of crushed ice in a blender, blend at medium speed for a few seconds, then at high speed until the mixture thickens. Pour into two chilled champagne glasses: finish with a cherry.

# Plantation Swizzle

| | | |
|---|---|---|
| 1¹/₂ oz | Aged Jamaican dark rum | 40 ml |
| 1 oz | Freshly squeezed lime juice | 30 ml |
| ¹/₂ tsp | Jamaican pimento dram liqueur | 2 ml |
| ¹/₂ tsp | ❖ Busha Browne's Spicy & Hot Pepper Sherry | 2 ml |
| 2 tsp | Confectioner's sugar | 10 ml |

Fill tall glass halfway with crushed ice. Pour over all ingredients and stir vigorously with a swizzle stick until frothy. Leave swizzle stick in glass and garnish with a sprig of fresh spearmint.

# Busha Browne's Rum Collins

Mix together in a tall heavy bottomed glass, 1¹/₂ oz (40 ml) aged Jamaican gold rum, ¹/₂ oz ( 15 ml) lime juice and 2 tsp (10 ml) powdered sugar. Add ice cubes and carbonated water. Stir and add cherry.

# Busha's Horse's Neck

| | | |
|---|---|---|
| 1 1/2 oz | Jamaican gold rum or brandy | 40 ml |
| 1 tsp | Freshly squeezed lime juice | 5 ml |
| 1/2 tsp | ❖ Busha Browne's Spicy & Hot Pepper Sherry | 2 ml |
| 1 | Thin slice fresh ginger root | 1 |
| | Dry ginger ale | |

Peel the skin of the lime around in one piece. Place over the edge of a tall glass to resemble a horse's neck. Fill glass three quarters full with ice cubes and pour over ingredients adding ginger ale last. Stir.

# Parliament Stinger

| | | |
|---|---|---|
| 3 oz | Brandy or Jamaican gold rum | 90 ml |
| 1 1/2 oz | White crème de menthe | 40 ml |
| 1 oz | Freshly squeezed lime juice | 30 ml |
| 1/2 tsp | ❖ Busha Browne's Spicy & Hot Pepper Sherry | 2 ml |
| 1/2 cup | Crushed ice | 125 ml |

Shake ingredients with ice and strain into two stemmed cocktail glasses.

# Kelly's Cow

| | | |
|---|---|---|
| 1 oz | Aged Jamaican dark rum | 30 ml |
| 1 oz | Jamaican coffee liqueur | 30 ml |
| | Fresh ice cold milk | |
| | Freshly grated nutmeg | |

Over ice cubes in a tall glass, pour the rum and the coffee liqueur. Fill with cold milk and stir. Top with freshly grated nutmeg.

# Cocoa Walks Caper

| | | |
|---|---|---|
| 1 oz | Jamaican coffee liqueur | 30 ml |
| 1/2 oz | Jamaican coconut rum liqueur | 15 ml |
| | Fresh unsweetened coconut water | |

Pour ingredients over ice cubes in a tall glass. Stir and top with freshly grated nutmeg and a wedge of coconut meat split to fit on edge of glass. VARIATION: *Carbonated water may be used if coconut water is not available, in which case, garnish with a sprig of mint.*

# Duppy Conqueror

In Jamaican parlance "Duppy Conqueror" means someone who is the biggest and the baddest. Bob Marley of reggae fame wrote a song with this title. A duppy is a ghost or spirit of the dead, derived from the African concept that man has two spirits or souls, one that goes to heaven to be judged while the other can linger on earth indefinitely and be manipulated for good or evil.

🌴 🌴 🌴

| | | |
|---|---|---|
| 1 oz | Jamaican white rum | 30 ml |
| 1 oz | Wild orange liqueur | 30 ml |
| 2 oz | Tamarind juice | 60 ml |
| ¼ tsp | Freshly grated ginger | 1 ml |
| Dash | ❖ Busha Browne's Pukka Hot Pepper Sauce | Dash |
| | Crushed ice | |
| | Carbonated water | |

Fill tall chilled glass ¾ full with crushed ice. Pour over all ingredients and stir. Top up with carbonated water and garnish with slice of orange.

# Busha's Pimento Julep

| | | |
|---|---|---|
| 3 oz | Aged Jamaican gold rum | 90 ml |
| ½ tsp | Jamaican pimento dram liqueur | 2 ml |
| 3 | Sprigs fresh spearmint | 3 |
| 1 tsp | Confectioner's sugar | 5 ml |
| 1 tbsp | Water | 15 ml |
| | Crushed ice | |

Chill silver julep goblet or tall glass. In bottom of goblet or glass, place two sprigs of the mint, the sugar and water. Muddle the mint and sugar with a long spoon until the mint is bruised. Fill ¾ full with crushed ice and pour over half the rum with the pimento dram. Stir vigorously until frost has begun to appear on goblet or glass and ice has dropped. Fill with more ice and the balance of the rum and stir. Garnish with sprig of mint and insert two short straws so that julep may be sipped from the top.

Tip: *Place the goblet or glass on several folds of dry newspaper. This will act as an insulator and will quicken the frosting process.*

# Tamarind Fizz

Mix 2 oz (60 ml) Jamaican wild orange liqueur and 4 oz (120 ml) pure thick tamarind juice. Pour over crushed ice in two tall chilled glasses and top up with carbonated water. If too tart, sweeten with granulated sugar.

# Moonshine Baby

"Moonshine Baby" refers to a traditional game that used to be
played by children in the country at the time of full moon.

| | | |
|---|---|---|
| 1 | Ripe banana, cut in pieces | 1 |
| 1 cup each | Guava nectar and orange juice | each 250 ml |
| 1 tbsp | Logwood honey | 15 ml |
| 1/2 cup | Ice cold milk | 125 ml |

Mix ingredients in blender until smooth. Add a cup (250 ml) of crushed
ice and serve from pitcher with a sprinkling of grated nutmeg.
VARIATION: *A derivative of this recipe is also known as "Nursery punch". Add
a cup of brandy and you have a punch fit for the Nursery Handicap at the Races.*

# Busha's Paw Paw Smoothie

| | | |
|---|---|---|
| 2 cups | Ripe paw paw, peeled and cubed | 500 ml |
| 2 cups | Freshly squeezed grapefruit juice | 500 ml |
| 1/3 cup | ❖ Busha Browne's Twice Boiled Guava Jelly | 80 ml |

Blend all ingredients in blender with a cup (250 ml) of crushed ice and
pour into two tall chilled glasses. Garnish with a sprig of mint.
VARIATION: *Different combinations can be used such as banana and mango
juice, soursop and orange juice, guava and passion fruit juice, etc..*

# Pineapple Flip

| | | |
|---|---|---|
| 2 cups | Fresh chilled pineapple or orange juice | 500 ml |
| 1 tbsp | Logwood honey | 15 ml |
| 1/2 tsp | ❖ Busha Browne's Spicy & Hot Pepper Sherry | 2 ml |
| 1 | Whole fresh egg | 1 |

Mix in blender with crushed ice. Serve in glasses with pineapple slices.

# Soursop Frappé

| | | |
|---|---|---|
| 2 cups | Freshly made chilled soursop juice | 500 ml |
| 2 tsp | Freshly squeezed lime juice | 10 ml |
| 1/2 tsp | ❖ Busha Browne's Spicy & Hot Pepper Sherry | 2 ml |
| 4 tbsp | Sweetened condensed milk or honey | 60 ml |
| 2oz | Jamaican gold rum (optional) | 60 ml |

Mix all and pour over crushed ice in tall glasses. Garnish with nutmeg.

# Busha Browne's Planter's Punch

This recipe is based on the long-standing rule for making Jamaican rum punch: "One of sour (lime), two of sweet (sugar), three of strong (rum) and four of weak (water)".

| | | |
|---|---|---|
| 1 cup | Freshly squeezed lime juice | 250 ml |
| 1 cup | Light brown sugar | 250 ml |
| 1 cup | ❖ Busha Browne's Twice Boiled Guava Jelly | 250 ml |
| 4 cups | Water | 1 l |
| 3 cups | Aged Jamaican gold rum | 750 ml |
| 1 tbsp | Jamaican pimento dram liqueur | 15 ml |
| 1/4 cup | ❖ Busha Browne's Spicy & Hot Pepper Sherry | 50 ml |
| 1/4 cup | Red maraschino cherries | 50 ml |
| | Freshly grated nutmeg | |

Put half the water in a saucepan. Add sugar and *Busha Browne's Twice Boiled Guava Jelly*, stirring over moderate heat until all has been completely dissolved. Cool syrup. Add lime juice, rum, pimento dram, pepper sherry and the rest of the water. Mix thoroughly and refrigerate. Makes 10 cups.

In an attractive punch bowl, place a large piece of ice that has been sealed in a plastic bag so that it will keep the punch cold without diluting. Pour the cold rum punch over ice: add cherries. Sprinkle grated nutmeg on top and ladle into punch cups or glasses adding a cherry to each one. VARIATION: *For a less potent brew, add 1 cup (250 ml) each orange juice, grapefruit juice, pineapple juice and passion fruit juice. Float thin slices of orange, pineapple and cherries.*

# St Jago Sangaree

This recipe comes from the Spanish brew, Sangria, and was particularly popular with the Jamaican plantocracy during the 18th century and beginning of the 19th century.

| | | |
|---|---|---|
| 2 bottles | Medium-dry red table wine or sherry | 2 bottles |
| 1 cup | Aged Jamaican gold rum or brandy | 250 ml |
| 8 cups | Freshly squeezed orange juice | 2 l |
| 1/2 tsp | Ground cinnamon | 2 ml |

Prepare a small orange by studding it all over with approximately 20 cloves. Freeze overnight. If possible, use a silver punch bowl. Seal a large piece of ice in a clear plastic bag and place in bowl to keep the brew cold without diluting. Mix wine, rum, orange juice and cinnamon together and pour over ice. Float the frozen orange studded with cloves on top. Slice another small orange, cut slices in half and arrange them around the whole frozen fruit. Ladle the well-chilled *Sangaree* into chilled goblets or glasses making sure that each glass has a slice of orange floating in it.

# Burns Café Jamaïque

Scotland's famous poet Robert Burns almost accepted a post as an overseer on a Jamaican estate in Portland. In 1786, Burns managed to publish a slim volume of poetry to help raise the £9 needed to pay his passage to Jamaica. He was on board the ship which was about to weigh anchor when a letter arrived to advise that his genius had finally been recognized.

| | | |
|---|---|---|
| 1 oz | Scotch whiskey | 30 ml |
| 1 oz | Aged Jamaican gold rum | 30 ml |
| 1/2 tsp | ❖ Busha Browne's Hot & Spicy Pepper Sherry | 2 ml |
| 2 tsp | ❖ Busha Browne's Twice Boiled Guava Jelly | 10 ml |
| | Jamaican Blue Mountain coffee | |
| | Freshly grated nutmeg | |

In a saucepan, warm the first four ingredients to melt the guava jelly. Pour into a prewarmed cup or, if preferred, a prechilled glass with crushed ice. Fill with piping hot, or cold, freshly brewed coffee. Stir in cream or top with whipped cream or ice cream. Sprinkle with grated nutmeg.

# Galway Goblet

Many immigrants, including the Browne/Sligo family, came to the New World from County Galway in West Ireland.

| | | |
|---|---|---|
| 1 oz | Irish whisky | 30 ml |
| 2 tsp | Dark brown sugar | 10 ml |
| 1/2 tsp | ❖ Busha Browne's Hot & Spicy Pepper Sherry | 2 ml |
| | Jamaican Blue Mountain coffee | |
| | Chilled whipped cream | |

Heat the first three ingredients in a saucepan but do not allow to boil. Pour into a prewarmed 7 oz goblet or coffee cup. Fill with very hot freshly brewed coffee and float chilled cream on top.

# Cinnamon Chocolata

As early as 1657, only two years after the British took Jamaica from the Spanish, shops were opened in London to sell chocolate beverages at luxury prices. Many of these popular gathering places later became famous clubs.

Mix in a saucepan 1/4 cup (60 ml) granulated sugar, 1/2 cup (125 ml) cocoa, and 1 tsp (5 ml) cinnamon. Stirring constantly, add 1 1/2 cups (375 ml) boiling water, bring to the boil then turn off heat. Add 3 cups (750 ml) scalded milk, 1 tsp (5 ml) vanilla, and 1/2 tsp (2 ml) *Busha Browne's Hot & Spicy Pepper Sherry*. Serve hot or cold with cinnamon stick. *The addition of 3 oz white crème de menthe or aged Jamaican gold rum is superbly delicious.*

# Busha Browne's Christmas Sorrel

As there is no winter in Jamaica, it is the maturing of the crimson sorrel bushes that indicates the coming of Christmas. Every Jamaican household has it special brew with bottles of the delicious bright red drink on hand for the festive season.

| | | |
|---|---|---|
| 8 cups | Sorrel sepals (2 lb) | 1 kg |
| 10 cups | Cold water | 2.5 l |
| 1 tbsp | Rice | 15 ml |
| 4 tbsp | Freshly grated ginger root | 60 ml |
| 10 | Pimento berries | 10 |
| 8 | Whole cloves | 8 |
| 2 cups | Granulated sugar | 500 ml |
| 2 oz | Aged Jamaican gold rum | 60 ml |

Place water, rice, grated ginger, cloves and pimento berries in a large non-reactive cooking pot. Bring to a rolling boil and drop in washed sorrel sepals. Turn off the heat, cover and let stand to steep for 24 hours. Strain off liquid into another container, add sugar and rum. Stir frequently until all sugar is dissolved. Decant into quart bottles and refrigerate to ripen for at least three days before using, longer is possible, as it improves with age. TIP: *Rice is used to start fermentation and rum is included as a preservative. More sugar and rum may be added according to personal taste.*

# Planter's Festive Egg Nog

| | | |
|---|---|---|
| 4 cups | Chilled fresh milk | 1 l |
| 4 | Fresh eggs | 4 |
| 1/4 cup | ❖ Busha Browne's Twice Boiled Guava Jelly | 60 ml |
| 1 tsp | ❖ Busha Browne's Spicy & Hot Pepper Sherry | 5 ml |
| 1/2 tsp | Grated orange rind | 2 ml |
| 3 oz | Aged Jamaican gold rum | 90 ml |
| 1 tsp | Freshly grated nutmeg | 5 ml |

Combine half of the milk with the other ingredients in blender until thoroughly mixed. Add balance of the milk, stir and refrigerate. Serve in punch bowl or glasses with sprinkling of freshly grated nutmeg on top.

# Busha's Any-time Shandy

Put 1/2 tsp (2 ml) Busha Browne's Spicy & Hot Pepper Sherry in the bottom of a tall chilled pilsner glass. Pour in equal parts of ice cold Red Stripe Beer and dry ginger ale. Shandy can also be served from a pretty punch bowl.

# Glossary

This Glossary provides, wherever appropriate, a description, historical notes, and an indication of what may be substituted. With reference to plants, fruits and vegetables, these can be regarded in their respective categories which correspond to the three principal historical periods of the island of Jamaica:

*Pre AD 1494   Taino period . . . (from about AD 600 to 1494)*

*1494 ~ 1655   Spanish period. . .(1494 ~ arrival of Columbus)*

*1655 ~ 1962   British period . . . (Conquest to Independence)*

The first recorded inhabitants of Jamaica are best referred to as 'Taino', being the name with which they described themselves to Christopher Columbus, meaning 'the good person (people)', rather than the more commonly used 'Arawak' which refers to their language still spoken by their descendants in northern South America.

The Taino of Jamaica were a highly organized and peace-loving people. Due to their superior agricultural skills, they were among the best nourished primitive communities in the world.

## ACKEE *Blighia sapida*

The national fruit of Jamaica though it is eaten as a vegetable. Grows on a beautiful medium sized tree which produces startling red to yellow fruit resembling small pears 3-4 in (7.5 - 10 cm). When ripe, the pod of the fruit bursts into three sections exposing three shiny black seeds, each attached to a yellow edible aril. A most decorative fruit and tree, it was introduced in 1778 from tropical West Africa. Captain William Bligh of the *Bounty* mutiny fame first took the plant from Jamaica to England where it was given its botanical name in his honour.

The ackee can be cooked in many ways; boiled with rice, in soufflés, or it may be fried when it assumes a nutty flavour. *Saltfish and Ackee* is a national dish in Jamaica and is much enjoyed by Jamaicans as well as visitors to the island.

The unripe ackee aril contains a poison (hypoglycin) and must therefore be properly picked and prepared and only eaten when just ripe and absolutely fresh. As a result, it is scorned by most of the world, indeed is banned in some countries. In Jamaica, almost every 'yard' has an ackee tree and no self-respecting Jamaican can do without his traditional Sunday morning savoury dish of *Saltfish and Ackee*.

There is no substitute. Seasoned scrambled eggs will have to suffice for the unfortunates who are unable to partake of this delectable food.

## AL DENTE

An Italian cooking term meaning cooked to the point of being firm and not overcooked. Literally the words translated mean 'to the tooth' and usually refers to cooking pasta and vegetables.

## ALLIGATOR PEAR (see AVOCADO)

## ALLSPICE (see PIMENTO)

## ALMOND *Terminalia catappa*

Almond nuts are produced from a handsome spreading tree that can attain a height of 40-50 ft (12-15 m) and thrives in the tropics including Jamaica from sea level to about 2,000 ft (600 m). The tree originated in India and is better referred to as the *Indian almond*. The true almond is the seed of *Prunus dulcis*.

## ANNATTO *Bixa orellana*

A small shrub native to Jamaica with tasteless seeds used to give a rich red colour to oil in which food is to be cooked. Annatto is a most decorative plant with clusters of brown to dark crimson ovoid pods with fleshy spines containing seeds with a crimson covering that provides a commercial red dye. This dye was the main pigment used as face and body paint by the Taino inhabitants of Jamaica.

Turmeric, which is also known as Indian saffron, can be used as a colouring agent in place of true saffron (*Crocus sativus*), the world's most expensive spice, which is highly esteemed and has its own distinctive fragrance and subtle flavour.

## ARROWROOT *Maranta arundinacea*

A white starchy flour that is obtained from the pointed root-like tubers of this attractive, low herbaceous plant. The tubers can also be eaten as a vegetable. Several varieties of arrowroot were cultivated by the Taino including varieties of another species *Canna indica* (Spanish or purple arrowroot). Both arrowroot and cornstarch may be used equally well as thickening agents:

$1^1/2$ *tsp (7 ml) arrowroot or cornstarch*

$= 1$ *tbsp (15 ml) plain flour*

Arrowroot flour must not be boiled or reheated and must be served immediately to hold. It does not have the raw taste of cornstarch or flour which can only be removed by cooking.

## ASPIC

A cold dish of meat, fish, vegetables and/or fruit combined and set in a gelatine mould.

## AUBERGINE *Solanum melongena*

Also known as *eggplant* or *garden egg* (in Jamaica) and a native of South Asia, the aubergine is one of the most decorative of vegetables with its spectacular shiny purple skin. It is eaten by itself boiled, baked or roasted or in stews and casseroles.

## AVOCADO *Persea americana*

In Jamaica familiarly called *pear*, *alligator pear* and *poor man's butter*, the avocado is one of the most popular fruits in the island though it is eaten as a vegetable. Native to Mexico and tropical America where it was first cultivated around 7000 BC, it is not certain if the avocado was growing in Jamaica prior to 1494 or if it was brought by the Spanish Conquistadores in the early 1500s while travelling to and from the Spanish Main.

There is no substitute for avocado though in Jamaica *pear* is used as a substitute for butter.

## BAMBOO *Bambusa vulgaris*

Bamboo is a part of the grass family as is sugar cane.

It is one of the most useful plants to man and is very beautiful. It has fibrous roots that bind the soil in mountainous places and on river banks. The tender shoots may be eaten and are frequently used in Chinese cookery. Originating in the Far East, it was probably introduced to Jamaica by the British after 1655. There are many other species of bamboo including a climbing type (*Chusquea abietifolia*) native to the Blue Mountains of Jamaica and to other West Indian islands.

## BAMMY

A thick delicious flat unleavened bread made from cassava (see page 105) flour that was an important element in the religious ceremonies of the Taino. A staple food in Jamaica for at least 1500 years, to this day bammy and its sister, the delicate cassava wafer, are still much enjoyed. Because of its excellent keeping qualities, the Spanish used Jamaican bammy to provision their ships travelling to and from the Spanish Main.

## BANANA   *Musa X paradisiaca*

Well known exported fruit of great economic importance to Jamaica where it is eaten both green and ripe. When green, it is boiled, fried, roasted or made into flour for porridge and is a nutritious and economical food. When used green, boiled or roasted, the banana skin should be cut at each end and scored deeply lengthwise with a knife to allow easy removal after cooking. In this way, the nutrients are better retained.

One of the very first foods enjoyed by man, the banana is believed by some to have been the *Tree of Knowledge* in the Garden of Eden. It originated in southern Asia but some authorities maintain that the banana was found in the Americas long before 1492. There is documentation that the Spanish brought the first cultivated banana to Jamaica in 1516. It is alleged that the botanical name *Musa* is derived from a legend that in olden days sages would lie beneath the shade of banana trees and eat the fruit while meditating. Bananas and plantains (see page 112) are all seedless hybrids of complex genealogy.

## BASIL   *Ocinum basilicum*

Also referred to as *sweet basil* and *l'herbe royal* this delicate herb with its fragrant and aromatic leaves is used to flavour soups, fish and egg dishes, and is especially good combined with tomato. It has long been considered a sacred herb to be planted near Hindu temples and, according to folklore, in one's garden to ensure happiness and harmony.

## BAY LEAF   *Pimenta racemosa*

The pungent bay leaf is dried and used sparingly to flavour soups, stews and casseroles and is one of the ingredients in a bouquet garni (see page 104). The aromatic evergreen leaves are borne on a medium, erect West Indian tree similar to *Pimenta dioica* and are used to make bay rum which is used medicinally similarly to rubbing alcohol.

Bay leaves also come from the bay laurel tree (*Laurus nobilis*) which is native to the Mediterranean. The stiff, glossy, aromatic leaves of this handsome tree were used in classical times as a sign of honour to make wreaths or crowns worn by conquerors, poets, Greek gods and Roman emperors as well as Olympic heroes. The first Olympic games of ancient Greece took place in 776 BC.

## BEANS   (see PEAS)

*Phaseolus vulgaris* (string beans, haricot)
*Phaseolus lunatus* (lima beans)

Referred to as a *pulse* which is the edible seed of certain pod-bearing plants such as *peas* and *beans*, the haricot or *string beans* as they are known in Jamaica, are eaten as a vegetable. If the pods are allowed to mature and become dry, *red peas* or *kidney beans* are the result.

Another variety is the flat lima bean eaten green as a vegetable or, in Jamaica, dried as an addition to stews etc. Both these beans were cultivated by the Taino pre AD 1494. Today they form an integral part of Jamaican cuisine and the dried string beans or red peas (kidney beans) are best known in Rice and Peas, one of the famous national dishes (see page 76).

## BÉCHAMEL

The French term for a white sauce made of butter, flour, milk or cream and seasonings. The spice mace is often used in béchamel sauce.

## BEES   *Apis mellifera*

The aggressive honeybee was brought to Jamaica by the Spanish and has since displaced most native bee species. It is not known if bee-keeping took place before 1534 when it is documented that honey was produced at Sevilla Nueva, the first Spanish capital at St Ann's Bay. It was here that Columbus first landed in Jamaica in 1494.

## BEETS OR BEETROOT   *Beta vulgaris*

Considered one of the most nutritious of root crops next to the potato, beets contain about 12 per cent sugar. Whether cooked or raw it is of great value as a vegetable as well as when used in salads.

## BELL PEPPER (see PEPPER)

## BLACK CRABS *Gecarcinus ruricola*
In his celebrated 1756 treatise on the *Civil and Natural History of Jamaica*, Patrick Browne, medical doctor, says of the Jamaican black crab: 'When the black crab is fat and in a perfect state, it surpasses every thing of the sort, in flavour and delicacy: and frequently joins a little of the bitter with its native richness, which renders it not only the more agreeable in general, but makes it sit extremely easy upon the stomach. They are frequently boiled and served up whole; but are commonly stewed when served up at the more sumptuous tables. . .'

The Jamaican black crab, a seasonal land crab that is actually dark red, should not be confused with the common Jamaican white land crab ( ) which is also edible. To this day the black crab is regarded by Jamaicans as a choice treat and these crabs are usually spicily prepared with loving care. Though not as delicate in flavour, sea crabs may be substituted.

## BLUE MARLIN *Makaira nigricans*
A large game fish, the Blue Marlin is found in Jamaican waters very close to the north shore of the island due to the great depth of water that descends into the Cayman Trench (see page 14).

## BOUQUET GARNI
A clever French invention; a small bunch of seasonings, including a bay leaf (see page 103) and herbs tied together or placed in a muslin bag used to flavour soups and stews. After cooking, the bouquet is removed and discarded.

## BREADFRUIT *Artocarpus altilis*
A favourite staple food in Jamaica that grows on a large, handsome, widespread tropical tree. Each fruit is round or oval, 5-7 inches (12-18 cm) long and has a curious rough green skin. It can be boiled, roasted or fried according to ripeness. The leaves of the tree are particularly decorative and have inspired many design artists.

The breadfruit originated in Polynesia and was brought to Jamaica in 1793 by Captain William Bligh of the *Bounty* mutiny fame.

Though quite different in flavour, potatoes or yams may be substituted for breadfruit.

## BULGUR
A parboiled dried cracked whole grain of wheat.

## BUSHA
Familiar Jamaican patois term used to address an owner, chief, headman or overseer of a plantation.

## CALABAZA *Cucurbita moschata*
Also known as *West Indian pumpkin*, calabaza is a member of the gourd, squash and melon family and has been a popular food cultivated in Jamaica since the time of the Taino. Calabaza pumpkin is eaten variably as a vegetable as well as in soups, stews, breads and sweet puddings.

The best substitutes are Hubbard, butternut and acorn squash which are not the same but are similar in colour and flavour.

## CALLALOO *Amaranthus viridus*
Though botanically considered a weed, callaloo is a form of greens easily and widely grown in Jamaica. It is a source of excellent nutriment and can be prepared in many ways. It is considered one of the principal Rastafarian foods, and is referred to as *ital* or *soul* food. (See RASTAFARIANISM page 113)

A native of the tropical Americas, this esteemed low herbaceous plant, along with many other edible species of wild callaloo, is common in Jamaica and was more than likely domesticated by the Taino prior to 1494.

Substitutes are all forms of spinach, Swiss chard, Chinese pak choy, etc., though none of them have the unique flavour of fresh young callaloo when it is properly prepared and promptly eaten .

## CAPER *Capparis spinosa*
A pickled flower bud used as a condiment from a shrub native to the Mediterranean region. There are several native species of *capers* in Jamaica.

## CASHEW *Anacardium occidentale*
A popular nut worldwide; the tree is a member of the mango family and produces an unusual edible, astringent acid 'fruit' (a fleshy enlarged 'receptacle' or modified stalk on which the nut is attached) that can be made into a delicious compote. The tree thrives in arid areas near the sea as well as to an elevation of 3,000 ft (900 m). The nuts, which are the actual fruit of the tree, must be roasted before they are eaten, otherwise they are poisonous.

A native of tropical America and the West Indies, the cashew tree was useful to the Taino inhabitants of the island who used it as a fruit, for oil, to make wine, as medicine and as a dye. An indelible 'ink' is produced from the sap of the cashew bark.

## CASSAREEP (see CASSAVA)

## CASSAVA *Manihot esculenta*
Also known as *manioc* and *yuca* the tuberous roots of the many varieties of *cassava* have been a starchy staple food from the earliest times. Cassava is more commonly known as *tapioca, farina* or *laundry starch*. These three are made from the bitter variety which is poisonous until it has been processed to remove the prussic acid. The sweet variety can be cooked and eaten as a starchy vegetable with impunity. Oddly enough the *bitter* and the *sweet* cassava both have the same name: taxonomically the two sorts are considered minor variants of a single species.

Cassava was much revered by the Taino who utilised it for ceremonial purposes and as one of their principal foods. They were extremely skillful in the cultivation and use of the different varieties of cassava from which they made bread or bammy (see page 103), beer, medicine, wound dressings and poisoned bait for hunting and fishing etc. Many of the Taino used the poisonous, uncooked bitter cassava juice to commit suicide in order to avoid being enslaved by the invading Spanish.

The same bitter cassava juice is the basis of the preservative *cassareep* also used by the Taino. *Cassareep* is the key ingredient in the pepperpot stew common to most West Indian islands apart from Jamaica. Jamaican *Pepper Pot* soup is quite different and *cassareep* has not been in general use in this island for over 150 years.

## CHO-CHO *Sechium edule*
Also known as *christophine* or *chayote* cho-cho is a perennial pear-shaped, light green vegetable that grows on a vine. It resembles *squash* or English *marrow* and has a pleasant bland taste when cooked. Raw, it is more flavourful and is excellent as a crudité and in salads. To this day the juice of the cho-cho is used medicinally in folk medicine to reduce hypertension. Cho-cho has similar tenderising properties to those of the paw paw (see page 111).

A native of tropical America it was brought to Jamaica by the Spanish in the 1500s.

## CILANTRO *Coriandrum sativum*
The dried seed of *cilantro* or *Chinese parsley* becomes the spice *coriander* which is much prized for making

curries, sausages, pickles or used in baked goods. Used fresh as cilantro the flavour has a totally different and unique characteristic which is specially appreciated in East Indian cuisine.

## CINNAMON *Cinnamomum zeylanicum*
Cinnamon is an essential spice that comes from the bark of a tree native to Sri Lanka (Ceylon - or Zeylan during that island's early Dutch period). Sri Lanka, an island slightly larger than Jamaica at similar latitude, and with similar climate and topography, is off the southern tip of India. The serendipitious introduction of the cinnamon tree to Jamaica took place in 1783 when Lord Rodney, ironically aboard *HMS Flora*, captured a French ship in Caribbean waters that was carrying various plants including cinnamon. Since then the spice has become popular in Jamaica as a flavouring for 'chocolate tea' (see COCOA page 106), in coffee (see page 107), cornmeal porridge, compotes, preserves, cakes and pastries to name but a few. The best cinnamon is recognized by sticks of thin layers of bark that are curled into each other. These must be ground at the last minute as powdered cinnamon loses its flavour quickly. The leaves are also used for oil and for flavouring infusions. (See MANGO page 110.)

## CITRUS FRUIT
### GRAPEFRUIT *Citrus X paradisi*
A large, yellow, much-acclaimed citrus fruit named for its habit of growing in clusters like grapes. Called 'the forbidden fruit' in the 18th century, it is believed to have been a hybrid of the sweet orange (*Citrus sinensis*) and the shaddock (*Citrus maxima*) and very likely originated in Jamaica.
### LIME *Citrus aurantifolia*
Small to medium green-skinned aromatic citrus fruit used widely in Jamaican cuisine for many dishes from the preparation of fish and meats to the seasoning of salads and vegetables as well as the making of desserts and beverages. A native of northern India, the fragrant lime was brought to Jamaica by the Spanish in the 1500s.
### ORANGE *Citrus aurantium*
Most citrus fruit derive from the sweet orange (*Citrus sinensis*) which originated in China and was brought to the Mediterranean by the Arabs. The Spaniards brought the Seville orange (sour orange - *Citrus aurantium*) to Jamaica in the early 1500s to make marmalade in order to provision their ships on the Spanish Main and to help prevent scurvy from afflicting their crews.

Since soon after the arrival of Columbus in 1494 to Jamaica many varieties of citrus have been grown and developed in the island, such as the grapefruit and the Temple orange now grown widely in Florida, the Ugli and the much prized Ortanique.

### ORTANIQUE

A unique cross between the orange and the tangerine which was developed in Jamaica during the early 1900s and has been widely exported ever since. In size and appearance, it is similar to a large flattened orange. It has few seeds, is very juicy with a deep orange colour, a beautiful aroma and a tangy/sweet flavour far superior to most other oranges.

### CLOVES *Syzygium aromaticum*

Also known as *clou de girofle* (French for 'nail of the clove tree'), the clove is a pungent spice and is the dried flower bud of a tropical tree native to South East Asia. Cloves were used in China over 2000 years ago and were favoured also by the Romans for medicinal purposes, as an antiseptic and to disguise the taste of rancid food. Cloves are to be used sparingly in curries, in pickling and marinades, in stewed fruits and marmalades and with meats such as ham. An onion studded with 3 or 4 cloves is a classic addition to stocks and stews.

## COAL POT

Footed open bowl-shaped iron cooking stove used to contain charcoal for an open fire.

### COCOA *Theobroma cacao*

Called *cocoa, chocolate tree* and *chocolate* in Jamaica, *cacao* is the plant from which commercial chocolate is derived. The seeds from its large pods are fermented and processed by roasting to make the 'chocolata balls' that can be grated to make Jamaican *chocolate tea* (otherwise known as the more familiar and much appreciated drink, cocoa). Jamaican cocoa is among the best grown in the world.

A native of tropical America, cocoa was brought to Jamaica for cultivation by the Spanish in the 1500s.

## COCOA WALKS

Name of one of the two Jamaican plantations in the old parish of St Dorothy (now part of St Catherine) that was the property of Howe Peter Browne, the 2nd Marquis of Sligo. (See SLIGO p. 114 and KELLY'S p. 109)

### COCO *Xanthosoma sagittifolium*

Also called *tania* and *yautia*; the *coco* or *soup coco*, as it

is known in Jamaica, is a starchy staple tuberous perennial with large handsome arrow-shaped leaves cultivated widely in tropical countries all over the world. It is native to tropical America and was cultivated by the Taino of Jamaica. The nutritious edible tubers are considered by some to be superior to Jerusalem artichokes and potatoes. There are two types, the other being *Colocasia esculenta* (see below). Though it does not have the same flavour or texture, the Irish potato (see page 113) may be substituted as a thickening agent for soups and stews.

### COCOE *Colocasia esculenta var. esculenta*

Also termed *dasheen, coco yam* and *taro*, this plant is similar to coco or *Xanthosoma sagittifolium* but is slightly smaller with broad heart-shaped leaves. It is similar to its cousin *Colocasia var. antiquorum*, otherwise known as *eddoe*. In some countries, the leaves as well as the tubers are eaten. The 'head' of the plant (at the base of the leaves) is also eaten. A native of tropical Asia, this is the esteemed *taro* of Hawaii and Polynesia and has been grown in Egypt from ancient times.

### COCONUT *Cocos nucifera*

The coconut is one of the most useful plants to man as it provides pure potable water, ready food, oil, wood and fibre. It plays an important role in Jamaican cookery and is one of the most romantic and attractive of trees. The fresh white 'meat' of the coconut is grated and used to make coconut milk (see page 20) or is shredded to make dessicated coconut for confectionery. The dried meat of the coconut is termed *copra* and is used for making oil.

Surprisingly, coconut oil is not only used for edible consumption. Among other things, it is the main ingredient of brake fluid and is the basis of the filler between layers of safety glass such as for windshields, etc. Coconut water comes from the fresh young green coconut and is not to be confused with the sweet liquid of the dry coconut which, in Jamaica, is discarded when the coconut is broken and before the dried meat is grated.

The characteristic Jamaica Tall coconut palm has been almost wiped out by the Lethal Yellowing disease and has been replaced by more resistant varieties since the first serious outbreak in 1961. The coconut has been used for making sugar, medicine, palm wine or arrack; for timber flooring, thatch, domestic utensils etc. by inhabitants of tropical areas for thousands of years.

## COCONUT MILK (see page 20)

## COCONUT WATER (see COCONUT page 106)

## CODFISH  *Gadus*
Known as *saltfish* in Jamaica, and as *bacalao* in Spanish speaking countries, nutritious dried salted (unrefrigerated) cod fish has been a staple food in the island for almost three hundred years.

## COFFEE  *Coffea arabica*
The world-renowned brew *coffee* has been grown in Jamaica since 1728 when it was introduced from Haiti by Governor Sir Nicholas Lawes. Today *Jamaica Blue Mountain* coffee commands the highest price in the world market, especially in Japan, and is used worldwide for its superior blending qualities. Coffee was first cultivated in Arabia from AD 575, went to Abyssinia (Ethiopia) in the early 1400s, thence to India in 1600, India to England in 1652, to Java in 1699 and to Amsterdam in 1706. In 1723 plants from the Paris Botanical Gardens were taken to Martinique. Of these only a single plant survived to provide plants for the entire Western Hemisphere and many other tropical areas of the world.

It should be noted that several other species are used for making the beverage such as *Coffea liberica* for Nescafé and *Coffea canephora* known as 'robusta'.

## COMPENDIUM
A short but complete summary, abstract or abridgement of something larger; compendium can also refer to a shortened collection.

## COMPOTE
A French term for fruit stewed or cooked in syrup served either hot or cold. It also means a long-stemmed dish for holding fruit, nuts, candy etc.

## CONCH  *Strombus gigas*
An Antillean gastropod mollusk having a large spiral shell with a bright shiny pink interior from which *cameos* are made. The 'meat' is extracted from the shell and is much prized for seafood chowder, soups and stews. Sea conch has been in use from the Taino period to the present.

## CONGO PEAS  *Cajanus cajan*
Another pulse (see BEANS page 103) the Congo peas, otherwise termed *pigeon peas* and in Jamaica called *gungo peas*, are excellent eaten green as a vegetable or dry cooked with rice etc. These peas/beans were introduced by the British after 1655 and probably originated in Africa.

## CORN OR MAIZE  *Zea mays*
Previously called *Indian Corn*, this well known cereal or grain is also eaten as a vegetable and is a member of the grass family with many varieties. Cornmeal, sometimes called *Indian meal*, was cultivated by the Taino and ground in a metate which was a form of mortar. To this day the very best cornmeal is stone ground.

Called *maiz* by the Taino people, corn was one of the commodities taken from the New World to the Old by the Spanish Conquistadores.

## CRUDITÉS
A French culinary term for raw vegetables.

## CURRY
*Curry* is the term given to the condiment that originated in India and is an art in itself. Some of the main ingredients are variably: ground coriander seeds, turmeric, fenugreek, ginger, black pepper, cayenne, cardamom, cumin, chilis, cinnamon, fennel, mustard, cloves and mace. Each cook's mixture is unique, according to area and custom, either as a dry powder or in paste form in which case onion and garlic are included. No two curries are alike.

## DILL  *Anethum graveolens*
Dill, or *dillweed*, is a popular herb used in the preparation of fish, vegetables and salads, etc. It is also used in dishes with sour cream and yogurt as well as for pickling the famous *dill pickle*.

## DUCKANOO
Originating from a West African dish, duckanoo is a spicy sweet plantain (see page 112) or cornmeal pudding prepared and cooked in a most original way. (see INTRODUCTION page 5 and page 79)

## EGGPLANT  (see AUBERGINE)

## EMANCIPATION
The abolition of slavery was proclaimed in the British Colonies on August 1, 1834 but absolute freedom was not achieved by the slaves until four years later. Howe Peter Browne, the 2nd Marquess of Sligo and Governor of Jamaica (1834-1836) was one of the proponents of emancipation. He was known in Jamaica as 'The Emancipator of the Slaves'. While slavery ended in Jamaica in 1838, it was not abolished in the United States of America until 1868, at the end of the Civil War.

## ESCALLION  *Allium fistulosum*

Otherwise known as *scallion* or *Welsh onion*, escallion is a member of the onion, garlic, chive family. It is similar to the spring onion but has a stronger flavour and is extensively used in Jamaican cooking with or without onion. Spring onions, garlic tops or fresh green onion tops may be substituted.

## ESCOVEITCHED FISH

A special spicy way of preparing fish inherited from Spanish Jews who took refuge in Jamaica in the early 1500s. (see INTRODUCTION and page 50)

## FESTIVAL

A savoury sweet cornmeal dumpling (see page 78).

## FLOUR

A soft fine powdery substance obtained by grinding and sifting the meal of a grain, especially wheat. Wheat flours are generally used for baking and have different names according to their different grades and mixes. They are variably called all-purpose flour in the USA, plain flour in Britain, counter-flour, cake-flour, self-rising flour etc. Non-wheat flours are also made from commodities such as corn (as a by-product of cornmeal/cornstarch), rice, soy, potato, cassava (tapioca), sago, arrowroot, green banana, plantain and many others.

## FRITTATA

A type of Italian omelette with a filling.

## GARDEN EGG  (see AUBERGINE)

## GARLIC  *Allium sativum*

Garlic is a condiment in the onion family, rich in Vitamins B, C and D that originated in central Asia. The green tops (like *chives*) can be used during the growing period. They dry when the garlic is mature. The bulbs consist of separate *cloves* and have to be reaped by hand, cleaned and cured by drying in sunlight. Garlic, with its pungent flavour, is one of the principal elements of Jamaican cuisine and has been well-known since antiquity for its medicinal qualities. It has variously been used raw as a cure for leprosy, hypertension, influenza, infections and skin conditions. It is still today in use as a natural antibiotic, a vermifuge and a fungicide. Though its strong odour is repugnant to some, garlic is unsurpassed as an enhancement to the cooking of a great many countries around the world.

## GINGER  *Zingiber officinale*

Ginger or *ginger root* is one of the oldest and most important of all spices. Jamaican ginger is highly prized in the world market. It is indigenous to tropical Asia, from China to India, and may also have been native to tropical South America. Ginger has an intriguing history and is documented from ancient times in Chinese and Indian literature as a spice used for a myriad of medicinal purposes. It is mentioned in the Talmud (Body of Jewish Law) and was used by the early Babylonians. It was popular in England long before the Norman Conquest, 1066 and was the principal ingredient in a remedy used during the Great Plague of London c 1347. During the 13th Century Marco Polo obtained ginger on his visit to both China and India and for centuries it was used for taxation purposes between the East and Europe.

It is documented that in 1525 ginger was brought via New Spain (Mexico) to Jamaica by the Spaniards. It is among the earliest commodities in continuous cultivation in Jamaica to this day and still commands the best world price, as does Jamaican coffee (see COFFEE page 107 and COCOA page 106).

In folk medicine, fresh ginger root is used as a stimulant, an expectorant and as a carminative. In cooking, it is unparalleled for imparting an exciting flavour to savoury and sweet dishes alike and is one of the essential ingredients for sauces, curries, chutneys, ginger beer, ginger ale, confectionery and with pimento (*allspice*) for jerking meats. (See JERK page 109 and page 70.)

## GIZZADA

Probably of Spanish-Jewish origin, small sweet tartlets made of pastry with a coconut filling.

## GUAVA  *Psidium guajava*

The guava, rich in vitamin C, is a succulent tropical fruit much appreciated for its unique flavour and preservability. It makes one of the best jellies, is excellent eaten raw or stewed as a compote and is equally delicious used as a jam or guava *cheese* (*guava dolce* - a coveted confectionery) in tarts and as a flavourful nectar drink.

A native of tropical America, including the island of Jamaica, guavas are about the size of small oranges and grow on a small spreading tree. When ripe they are usually yellow outside, while inside the soft edible skin, the sharp, tart pulp is pink and has many seeds. The fruit has a large percentage of natural pectin, which is the substance that causes the boiled jelly (with sugar) to set or jell (congeal). In the best jellies, no gelatin is used to 'stretch' the jelling capability of the extracted fruit juice.

Guava was cultivated as a fruit by the Taino of Jamaica who also used it medicinally for diarrhoea, diabetes and hypertension.

## HARD-DOUGH BREAD

A dense white or wholewheat bread, made commercially in Jamaica. It is now much sought after in Jamaican specialty shops worldwide.

## HONEY (see BEES)

## HOWE PETER BROWNE (see SLIGO)

## IRIE

A Rastafarian term meaning the state of being at one with nature and at peace with oneself and all things, including one's brother man. (See RASTAFARIANISM page 113.)

## ITAL

A Rastafarian term denoting natural vegetarian dishes cooked without salt or other additives. (See RASTAFARIANISM page 113.)

## JAMAICA

*Xaymaca* in the Arawak language (which means 'the land of wood and water')is a very hospitable island of 4,411 square miles (1,704 square km) in area, 144 miles (230 km) long and 52 miles (83 km) at the widest point. It is the third largest island in the Caribbean after Cuba and Hispaniola (Haiti and the Dominican Republic) which are its closest neighbours. Blue Mountain Peak at an altitude of 7,402 feet (2,243 m) surveys the rugged mountainous backbone of the island that runs almost in line with the 18th degree of latitude North, south of the Tropic of Cancer at 23°. With its dignified people, idyllic climate and varied topography, Jamaica might be considered a most beautiful, bounteous and beneficial country.

## JERK

The term *jerk* refers to a form of grilling or barbecuing meat, especially pork. This culinary specialty has become an art form in Jamaica where it has been widely practiced for some 400 years. (See MAROONS page 110 and page 70)

## JONGA (JANGA) *Macrobrachium carcinus*

*Jonga* is the Jamaican patois name for freshwater crayfish which are crustaceans resembling a smaller version of the spiny lobster. There are several species in Jamaica. The smaller 'peppered' version frequently sought after at Middle Quarters by connoisseurs goes by the fomidable name *Macrobrachium acanthurus*. (See pages 47 and 54.)

## JULIENNE

A French cooking term meaning to cut into thin strips about 2-3 in (5 -7 cm) long by 1/8 in (.5 cm) in thickness. Vegetables can be cut in this way for interest and variety. This fancy cut is also called *jardiniere* and *allumette* (matchsticks).

## KELLY'S

*Kelly's* is the name of a Jamaican plantation in the old parish of St Dorothy (now part of St Catherine) that was the property of Howe Peter Browne, the 2nd Marquis of Sligo. (See SLIGO page 114 and COCOA WALKS page 106.)

## KINGFISH *Scomberomorus cavalla*

A very large fish attaining weights of up to about 80 lb (36 kg), Kingfish is generally cut into steaks and is steamed or escoveitched. This fish is frequently confused with another game fish the *Wahoo* that goes by an equally ponderous name *Acanthocybium solanderi*.

## LIMA BEANS

A pulse also known as *broad* beans or *butter* beans. (See BEANS page 103)

## LIME (see CITRUS FRUIT)

## LOBSTER (SPINY LOBSTER) *Panulirus argus*

Known elsewhere as *langouste* and *rock lobster*, the *spiny lobster* found in Jamaican waters is a marine decapod crustacean and is not to be confused with the genus *Homerus* which has large claws or pincers and is found in northern waters. The langouste's Mediterranean cousin uses the scientific name *Palinurus vulgaris*.

## LOVE-APPLE (see TOMATO)

One of the products found in the New World, the tomato has had a chequered past being considered alternately both poison and aphrodisiac. Both red and yellow tomatoes have been known variously as *Pomme d'amour* by the French, *Amorous Apples* by the English and *Pomodori* (golden apples) by the Italians. It is thought that the word is derived from *pomo de Mori*, Italian for *Moorish apple* which recalls that the tomato was brought to the Old World by the Spanish.

## MACE (see NUTMEG)

An important spice and a by-product of the nutmeg being the net-like wrapper (aril) surrounding the nutmeg husk with the nut or kernel itself inside the encapsulated husk.

## MAMMEE APPLE  *Mammea americana*

Also known as *St Domingo Apricot*, this unusual and hard to find fruit is a member of the *Mangosteen* family and is native to Jamaica and tropical America. The handsome medium-sized tree is a slow-growing evergreen, with large leathery, shiny dark green leaves. The fruit is nearly spherical 4-7 in (10-17 cm) in diameter with a thick, rough brown skin, and a distinct nipple towards the apex, from which it derives its name. Each fruit has one or two large seeds embedded in a dense bright orange, sweetish and slightly aromatic pulp which can be eaten raw or stewed for a compote or tart filling. The scented flowers are distilled to make the liqueur *Eau-de-Creole*. Mammee apple can only be compared to a cross between the mango, the peach and the apricot. It has been thought by some to be poisonous but, like many other foods, it can be mildly toxic to individuals sensitive to certain organisms.

## MANGO  *Mangifera indica*

The fragrant mango is one of the most prized and romantically exotic of fruits and has been cultivated since pre-historic times. A native of tropical Asia, the most flavourful mangos grown in Jamaica are the Bombay, the St Julien and the East Indian. There are now many other commercial derivatives exported, but none compare to the less exploited varieties including the common *Black* mango and the *Number 11* which are especially good when used in chutneys. *Number 11* was brought to Jamaica in 1782 by Lord Rodney whose squadron captured a French ship bound from Mauritius to Haiti with many plants on board. (See CINNAMON page 105)

## MARLIN (See BLUE MARLIN)

## MAROONS

The word Maroon comes from the Spanish word 'cimarron' which means wild or untamed, living on the mountain tops. In Jamaica, Maroon refers to a special group of people who after much struggle, fighting and eventual peace treaties, to this day enjoy autonomy in their private government within the jurisdiction of the island of Jamaica.

In the early 1500s, at the beginning of the Spanish occupation of Jamaica, Moorish men were brought from Spain to be employed as security guards and tenders of cattle by the Spanish garrison. The Jamaican Maroons are descended from a mixture of these Moorish men, Spanish soldiers, African men of the Ashanti Guard who were kidnapped to Jamaica in the early 16th century and Taino women.

Contrary to popular belief, the Jamaican Maroons were never slaves. At the time of the British conquest in 1655, these proud and indomitable people hid in the mountains to avoid being taken as slaves. In their fierce pursuit for freedom, the Maroons outsmarted the British until 1795 after which time the treaties previously agreed were finally accepted by both sides.

The Maroon tradition is the only continuous element that weaves through Jamaica's history from the post-Columbian era to the present time.

During the years of the *Maroon Wars*, the Maroons were forced to subsist in the mountains on wild hog, available plants and ground provisions. Their special way of jerking (barbecuing) meat has become an important feature of traditional Jamaican cookery. (See pages 69, 70 and 71)

## MOLASSES (see SUGAR)

A by-product of cane sugar used in cooking.

## MUTTON

Lamb is often referred to as mutton. In Jamaica mutton is much esteemed goat meat.

## NUTMEG  *Myristica fragrans*

The nutmeg, also known as *nois muscade*, is an important spice from ancient times used for every type of cooking and medicine imaginable. A native of the Molucca Islands (formerly Spice Islands) near New Guinea in Indonesia, the medium sized nutmeg tree is evergreen and a beautiful specimen plant in a garden. Usually dioecious (having male and female flowers borne on separate plants) this tree was probably introduced by the British at the same time to both Jamaica and Grenada, the latter known today as 'The Nutmeg Isle'.

The pale amber whole fruit, about the size of an apricot, is spectacularly decorative, especially when it splits open to reveal the nutmeg itself encapsulated by a bright scarlet, net-like aril which is another spice, *mace* (see above). When reaped, the mace should be allowed to dry naturally in a shady place before removal from the shell. The outer shell of the nut of the nutmeg should remain intact until required, when it is cracked open and the kernel is freshly grated to release the nutmeg's subtle aroma and somewhat musky flavour.

Like many other exotic Asian spices, the nutmeg has been one of the main incentives for world exploration and also the subject of much medical speculation. Ferdinand Magellan captured the lucrative nutmeg trade in the Moluccas for the Portuguese in 1512. Nutmeg was considered to be a powerful antidote for plague and was used in Indian and Arabic medicine from over a thousand years ago. In the early 1700s, nutmeg was a major fad causing people to carry the nuts around their necks in a special contrivance (made of silver, ivory, wood or bone) that incorporated its own grater. As early as 1576, the hallucinogenic properties of the nutmeg were documented as a result of the belief that the eating of 10-12 nutmegs would cause a miscarriage; a misconception that has endured with less educated peoples to this day. *Myristicin*, the psychoactive element in nutmeg was only isolated around the turn of this century. It is important to understand that 'overdosing' on nutmeg can actually cause death.

## OKRA  *Abelmoschus esculentus*
Sometimes referred to as *ladies fingers* or *gumbo* the okra is a mucilaginous vegetable eaten on its own or in soups and stews, as a thickening agent and to impart a delicate flavour. As with most members of the hibiscus family, the flowers are somewhat oily and are excellent, surprising as it may seem, for polishing shoes and other leather items; thus the common name 'shoe-black' as the many beautiful flowering varieties of hibiscus are known in Jamaica.

## ONION  *Allium cepa*
A very popular root vegetable found in various forms and colours all over the world. The purple or Spanish red onion is a mild, sweet onion.

## ORTANIQUE  (see CITRUS FRUIT)

## PAK CHOY  *Brassica rapa var. chinensis*
Also known as Chinese Cabbage, pak choy is a member of the mustard/turnip family.

## PASSION FRUIT  *Passiflora maliformis*
In Jamaica, the native purple variety, *Passiflora maliformis*, is known as *sweet cup* while the larger yellow variety (*Passiflora laurifolia*) is called *golden apple*. Native to southern Brazil it has been growing in Jamaica for 'donkey's years' along with its larger sister, granadilla (*Passiflora quadrangularis*). All varieties are used for a delicious and refreshing drink or for ice cream and sherbets or hot weather desserts and nectars.

## PATTY
A popular snack in Jamaica, patties are minature, crescent shaped pies with a seasoned meat filling similar to an English pasty. Made smaller, they become *cocktail patties*, while filled with sweetened spicy plantain purée they become *plantain tarts*.

## PAW PAW  *Carica papaya*
Papaya, known as *paw paw* in Jamaica, is one of the most unusual plants known to man. In its more familiar ripened state, it is a nourishing and delicious bright orange fruit similar to a melon. Green, it can be julienned for salad and, younger and greener still, it can be cut up in stews and curries or boiled and baked as any other vegetable. The spicy black seeds, with a sharp flavour somewhat like watercress, are used as a condiment in West Africa and are delicious in salad dressing (see page 34). Dried and ground, the seeds make an interesting health-food 'pepper'.

The highly esteemed paw paw is rich in the digestive protein enzyme *papain* (a vegetable pepsin) which promotes digestion. Taxidermists put small animals inside paw paw fruit to let the proteolytic enzymes clean up the skeletons! This most attractive plant is hard to define as either a herb, a shrub or a tree. All parts of the 'tree' contain tenderizing properties; thus tough meat wrapped in paw paw leaves before cooking will become tender.

The latex from the paw paw is used widely in medicine today as it was in the days of the Jamaican Taino who used it to aid digestion, and also to treat worms, diabetes, backache and hypertension. The 'tree' is dioecious (having male and female flowers borne on separate plants) and/or hermaphrodite, and is the subject of much humorous speculation including the folklore belief that a paw paw tree planted beside the window of a delinquent husband will sap his potency. In India the pawpaw has been used for centuries as an abortifacent.

The endemic wild Jamaican paw paw has the scientific name *Carica jamaicensis*, is found only in Jamaica and is not the same as the cultivated plant that was introduced during Jamaica's Spanish period.

## PEANUT  *Arachis hypogaea*
The lowly peanut, sometimes called *groundnut*, much enjoyed to this day, is an extremely nutritious food which was cultivated in Jamaica by the Taino who also used it as an aphrodisiac.

## PEAS  (see BEANS and SNOW PEAS)
A pulse. In Jamaica the term peas is interchangeable with the word beans. (See RICE & PEAS, page 76)

## PEPPER (see SCOTCH BONNET)

The coveted pepper that Columbus hoped to find on his several voyages was *Piper nigrum* or *black* pepper. What he did find and bring back to the Old World was hot *capsicum* or *chili* peppers.

Hot peppers, which are all members of the genus *Capsicum*, are known to have titilated the human diet for some 9,000 years. They are considered a fruit and are related to the aubergine (a native of southern Asia) as well as to the potato, tomato, and tobacco, products of the New World introduced by the Spanish to the Old World. The Taino would have brought hot peppers with them in their migration from the northern part of South America nearly 2,000 years ago.

Over the centuries, the many varieties of hot peppers (all teeming with Vitamins A and C) have been much prized and thought to have aphrodisiac as well as curative powers for ailments as diverse as arthritis, epilepsy, ulcers, hair loss, the common cold and to guard against spirits.

Sweet peppers, *Capsicum grossum*, (red, green or yellow bell peppers) are of the same family, are mild in taste, and are universally used in cookery.

## PEPPER POT

In Jamaica, the term pepper pot refers to a very popular and well-known spicy soup (see page 21).

## PIMENTO *Pimenta dioica*

Familiarly called *allspice* or *Jamaica Pepper* this exceptional spice is grown almost exclusively in Jamaica where it was in use by the Taino before 1494. It is called *allspice* because the flavour is said to be a combination of cinnamon, nutmeg and cloves. The tree is particularly handsome with glossy aromatic evergreen leaves (from which an essential oil is extracted) and has a smooth, light coloured almost barkless trunk. Every part of the tree is aromatic with a unique pungent fragrance pleasing to humans but obnoxious to insects. The spice comes from the green berries that resemble black pepper when dried. *Pimento dram* liqueur is made from the ripe berries while the famous Jamaican *jerk* barbecue depends for its flavour on being cooked over the aromatic pimento wood and leaves which imparts the irresistible smokey savour that was a speciality of the intrepid Jamaican Maroons (see MAROONS).

## PIMENTO DRAM (see PIMENTO)

A cordial used as a liqueur for after dinner or to flavour food. Also used medicinally.

## PINEAPPLE *Ananas comosus*

The pineapple is known the world over as the symbol of hospitality. A form of wild pineapple was growing in Jamaica at the time of the Taino who used it as food, wine, medicine for urinary complaints and to cause miscarriages; to make rope and cloth along with sea island cotton (*Gossypium hirsutum* used to treat asthma) which they spun and wove to make their extra special and much appreciated invention, the *hammock*.

Columbus took the pineapple, a native of tropical America, from the island of Guadeloupe to Spain in 1493 and from thence brought it back to the other West Indian islands to be cultivated.

Today, Hawaii is the largest commercial producer of pineapples but Jamaica has the distinction of having provided the Smooth Cayenne variety on which Hawaii bases its lucrative pineapple industry. In 1886, an English horticulturist, Captain John Kidwell imported 1,000 plants from Jamaica and later the Smooth Cayenne was acknowledged by researchers to be the best commercial variety.

## PITA BREAD

A flat round unleavened bread of Middle-Eastern origin made with white or whole wheat flour.

## PLANTAIN *Musa X paradisiaca* (see BANANA)

A variety of the banana, the plantain looks like a large, horn shaped banana but must be cooked before being eaten green or ripe. It has been a staple vegetable in Jamaica since the days of the Spanish.

In his definitive 1707 *Natural History of Jamaica*, the English physician/naturalist Sir Hans Sloane (1660-1753) describes plaintain leaves used as 'table cloths and napkins' by the inhabitants.

Sloan, known as 'the Jamaica doctor', spent 15 months in the island as the personal physician to the Duke of Albemarle (Governor 1687-1688) where he documented over 800 mostly new species of plants. In 1727 Sloane became the personal physician to George II and later became the founder of the British Museum by virtue of the bequest of his entire collection of botanical specimens and over 50,000 books and manuscripts.

## PONE

A term used in Jamaica for a cake or pudding made with sweet potato, cornmeal, sugar and spices and in olden days baked in an iron 'pone pot'. The word pone comes from the North American Indians and is documented in Jamaica by the

Jamaican historian Edward Long as early as 1774. In the United States pone refers to a kind of bread made from corn (maize).

## POTATO *Solanum tuberosum*
Called *Irish potato* in Jamaica and *English potato* in Barbados, the potato originated in the Peruvian Andes and was introduced to Europe by the Spaniards with the tomato and other plants.

## PULSE (see BEANS and PEAS)

## PUMPKIN (see CALABAZA)

## QUENELLE
A French culinary term for a ball or dumpling of forcemeat (or minced meat) bound with eggs that is usually poached in stock or water.

## QUICHE
French for a custard dish baked in a savoury pastry shell, often with bacon and/or cheese.

## RAISINS
Also known as *sultanas*, raisins are dried grapes that retain a large amount of natural sugar.

## RASTAFARIANISM (see INTRODUCTION page 5)
Rastafarianism is a religious philosophy concerning nature which originated in Jamaica in the early 1900s. As a cultural force, the movement has been gaining popularity worldwide mainly as a result of the creative genius of the late Bob Marley (1945-1981) who also popularised Reggae music. The bright Rastafarian colours are particularly significant:

Red ~ for the Blood;
Green ~ for the Earth;
Gold ~ for the Sun.

Ital (see page 109) is a Rastafarian form of all natural vegetarian cooking of products from the earth without using added salt or preservatives of any kind. Lime juice is used instead of salt along with hot peppers for seasoning.

Irie (see page 109) is the state of being at one with nature as well as being at peace with oneself and all things, including one's brother man.

## RED PEAS (see PEAS and BEANS)

## RED STRIPE BEER
Jamaica's own beer brewed in the island and a winner of many international medals and prizes.

## ROTI
A flat, round unleavened bread which, in the West Indies, is generally made by the descendants of East Indian immigrants.

## RUM
Rum, called *Kill Devil* when first made in the 1600s and later called *rumbullion*, is made from sugar cane and is one of the most important and renowned commodities exported from the island of Jamaica. Jamaica *gold* (light) rum is the most famous while *dark* rum is especially good for punches. *White* overproof rum is the drink of the populace and has long been used for medicinal purposes (inside *and* outside the body) as well as for religious and other rituals or ceremonies.

## SAFFRON *Crocus sativum*
A plant of the *Iris* family and also the name of the most expensive spice in the world. The plant is native to Asia, and has been cultivated for centuries for the aromatic orange-yellow stigmas or pistils, from which is made a dye and a flavouring that is popular in Mediterranean and Indian cooking (e.g. in curries). It requires approximately 4,000 flowers to produce 1 oz of Saffron powder.

## SALSA
A spicy, tart or sweet accompaniment, a cross between a condiment and a salad, usually made from a combination of vegetables and/or fruits with different piquant seasonings. *Salsa* is also the name of a type of popular music from Puerto Rico.

## SALT FISH (see CODFISH)

## SAMBALS
It is said that hot spicy foods (such as curries) cool the body. They should always be served with chutneys, pickles, relishes, cooling fruit and/or vegetable side dishes called SAMBALS (see page 67).

## SCOTCH BONNET *Capsicum chinensis*
The flavourful and *very* hot Scotch Bonnet pepper *Capsicum chinensis* is widely used in Jamaica and obtained its name due to its squashed appearance reputed to resemble the soft beret worn by Scotsmen. Since 1912 the 'hotness' of a pepper has been measured by the subjective Scoville Organoleptic Heat Test invented by one Wilbur Scoville. A hot jalapeño weighs in at 2,500-3,000 Scovilles, while the extra hot Scotch Bonnet tops the heat scale at 200,000 to 300,000 Scovilles!

## SHALLOTS  *Allium cepa var. aggregatum*

A relative of the onion, escallion and garlic, the shallot is used for seasoning as is garlic though it is not as strong in odour or flavour. The bulbs are small and red. When dried and hung in clusters they are most decorative.

## SHRIMP  *Penaeus*

Also called prawns, the many varieties of shrimp are marine decapod crustaceans that are sought after for their succulent meat and easy preparation.

## SLIGO

Howe Peter Browne (1788-1845), the second Marquis of Sligo, was Governor of Jamaica from 1834-36 and was popularly known in both Jamaica and Ireland as *'The Emancipator of the Slaves'*. (See INTRODUCTION page 4)

The seat of the Marquess of Sligo is Westport House which, oddly enough, is situated in County Mayo, adjacent to County Sligo, in Ireland.

## SNAPPER  *Lutjanus*

A large family of well-known bottom-feeding tropical marine fish that live on reefs, offshore banks and some in mangrove lagoons.

The Caribbean Red Snapper is *Lutjanus purpureus* while the even better known Yellowtail Snapper is inconveniently in a different genus and is called *Ocyurus chrysurus*. Nowadays it is all the more confusing as the freshwater red *Tilapia* (*Oreochromis*) is erroneously termed snapper.

## SNOW PEAS  *Pisum sativum*

Also known as *Mange-tout* and *sugar peas*, these are young, immature green peas which are eaten with their succulent pods as an extra special vegetable, especially in Chinese cuisine.

## SORREL  *Hibiscus sabdariffa*

This extremely unusual plant is also known as *Rozelle* and *Flor de Jamaica* (see page 100). An annual shrub, sorrel always matures in December when daylight is at its shortest period. When ripe, the stems and fleshy flower pods (sepals) become bright crimson. With the leaves removed, the stems and Japanese-lantern-type pods make an unrivaled floral decoration that will last 2-3 weeks and then may still be used to make the traditional holiday drink so much loved by Jamaicans. It can also be made into a jelly. Native from India through Malaysia, sorrel was introduced to Jamaica by the British soon after 1655.

## SOURSOP  *Annona muricata*

A native of Jamaica, the strange, succulent and prickly green soursop fruit, also known as *guanábana*, was cultivated by the Taino as a food and as medicine to aid fever, diarrhoea, labour, lactation, worms, indigestion and nausea. Soursop makes a marvellous tart/sweet cooling drink as well as great ice cream and should have a much wider audience as it is easy to grow and bears prolifically. The laurel-like leaves are also particularly fragrant.

## SPINY LOBSTER  (see LOBSTER)

## STAMP & GO

The Jamaican name for a special way of preparing codfish or saltfish fritters (see page 15).

## STAR APPLE  *Chrysophyllum cainito*

A native of Jamaica and the Greater Antilles, the star apple is a curious and delightful succulent round fruit about the size of an orange. Most often Star Apples have an outstanding shiny purple skin but they are also sometimes green: but green or purple, all are are equally delicious.

Inside, the fruit has transparent jelly-like segments that, when cut crosswise, reveal an eight pointed star embedded in a juicy pulp with a milky appearance.

The star apple tree is particularly beautiful, medium-sized and evergreen with characteristic dark green leaves on top and irridescent copper underneath which give the tree a striking appearance when blown in the breeze. It is a superb specimen plant in a garden. There is always a battle to prevent birds from enjoying the fruit before reaping time which is awkward as the fruit never drops off the tree and is difficult to pick. As a result, obstinate people in Jamaica are often referred to as being 'stubborn like star apple'. A traditional dessert called *matrimony* is made with fresh star apple and orange segments.

## SUGAR

Cane for sugar is grown extensively in Jamaica and provides the various sugars as well as Jamaica's renowned rum (see page 113), *molasses* (see page 110), and other by-products. American *granulated* sugar is finer than the English version, while English *castor* sugar is closer to American *powdered* sugar. *Confectioner's* sugar is the same as *powdered* sugar or *icing* sugar as it is termed in Europe.

In Jamaica, a dark brown sugar which retains

a hint of molasses is obtainable. This adds a distinctly different flavour and texture to dishes prepared with this heavy sugar. If so desired, add a tablespoon of molasses to dishes in which 'dark brown sugar' is specified, particularly in JAMAICAN PLUM PUDDING (see page 88).

## SWEET PEPPER *also* BELL PEPPER (see PEPPER)

## SWEET POTATO *Ipomoea batatas*
A tasty and nutritious staple food that was widely cultivated by the Taino of Jamaica who also made a type of beer from the tubers. There are an exceptional number of varieties in Jamaica.

## TAINO *(ARAWAKS)*
The Taino (popularly but incorrectly referred to as Arawaks) were the first recorded inhabitants of the island of Jamaica (see page 101).

## TAMARIND *Tamarindus indica*
Tamarinds are brownish pods containing a sweetish acid brown pulp used for making cooling drinks, as folk medicine and as one of the principal ingredients in chutneys and brown sauces. The tree is most decorative with its fine-leafed foliage but it is also very messy when the myriad pods drop off the trees and ferment on the ground.

## THYME *Thymus vulgaris*
Used widely in soups, with meats, in sauces and stuffing, this scented herb is also a most decorative rock garden and herbaceous border plant.

## TIMBALE
A French term for a custardlike dish made of cheese, chicken, fish or vegetables baked in a drum or thimble shaped mould .

## TOMATO *Lycopersicon esculentum*
A well-known fruit used as a vegetable which is important to the cuisine of most countries in the world (see LOVE-APPLE).

## TURMERIC *Curcuma longa*
A member of the *Zingiberaceae* family similar to ginger. The root of this tropical, perennial herb yields a yellow dye and is often used with ginger and cardamom seeds as a basis for curry.

## TURNED CORNMEAL
A savoury dish much enjoyed in Jamaica made with cornmeal and seasonings. Its rival polenta, much esteemed in Italy, is usually made of maize or cornmeal or from chestnut flour.

## VANILLA *Vanilla planifolia*
A large, climbing orchid, the vanilla plant has long, elliptic fleshy leaves and a curiously beautiful growth pattern on tree trunks or walls. The long thin brown vanilla beans were dried and cured by the Aztecs long before Columbus's arrival in the New World. A vanilla bean buried in a container of granulated sugar will quickly permeate the sugar with its special flavour. Vanilla may have been introduced to Jamaica from South and Central America by the Spanish. Outside of its native area, the vanilla flowers must be pollinated by hand, as they are fertile for only a short period.

## WATER CHESTNUT *Trapa bicornis*
A low aquatic floating plant bearing a two horned nut that is pickled in brine and used widely in Chinese and Indian cooking.

## WATER CRESS *Nasturtium officinale*
A low perennial herb commonly met on river banks or in swampy situations. It belongs to the mustard family and is not to be confused with the garden nasturtium (*Tropaeolum majus*) from which both leaves and flowers are edible and, like water cress, are excellent used as a salad greens.

## YAM *Dioscorea*
Yam is a much prized herbaceous, creeping trailing perennial requiring support that produces succulent tuberous roots which form an excellent tasting and nutritious food. These yams are not sweet and should not be confused with a variety of sweet potato grown in the United States of America also called 'yam'. There are many varieties including three favourites: *white* yams (*Dioscorea alata* and varieties), *yellow* yams (*Dioscorea cayennensis*), and the smaller *yampee* (*Dioscorea trifida*). All three are delicious boiled or roasted. A curious feature of these plants is that the stems of the *white* and *yellow* yam varieties always twine counter-clockwise while the stems of the yampee always twine clockwise.

## ZUCCHINI *Cucurbita pepo var.*
Also known as *courgette*, dark green zucchini is a prized member of the summer squash family which are all thin skinned regardless of shape, size or colour as against winter squash and pumpkin that have hard shelled skins. Zucchini should not be confused with certain types of cucumber. ❖

# Tables

To assist with the use of this cookbook, both American Standard and Metric measurement have been included. Approximate equivalent comparative tables, including Imperial measurement, have been devised to facilitate cooks from all over the world. The cup referred to throughout the book is the 8 oz American Standard cup or 250 ml while the teaspoon holds 5 ml and the tablespoon 15 ml etc.

| APPROXIMATE LIQUID MEASUREMENTS | | | | | | |
|---|---|---|---|---|---|---|
| Standard Measurement | | | Metric Measurement | | Imperial Measurement | |
| Spoons | Cups | Fluid Ozs | Millilitres | | Spoons/Cups | Fluid Ozs |
| 1/8 tsp | | | .5 ml | | 1/8 tsp | |
| 1/4 tsp | | | 1 ml | | 1/4 tsp | |
| 1/2 tsp | | | 2 ml | | 1/2 tsp | |
| 3/4 tsp | | | 4 ml | | 3/4 tsp | |
| 1 tsp | | | 5 ml | | 1 tsp | |
| 1 1/2 tsp | | | 7 ml | | 1 1/2 tsp | |
| 2 tsp | | | 10 ml | | 2 tsp | |
| 1 tbsp | | 1/2 oz | 15 ml | | 1 tbsp | 1/2 oz |
| 2 tbsp | 1/8 cup | 1 oz | 30 ml | | 2 tbsp | 1 oz |
| 3 tbsp | | 1 1/2 oz | 40 ml | | | |
| | | | 45 ml | | 3 tbsp | |
| 4 tbsp | 1/4 cup | 2 oz | 60 ml | | | |
| 6 tbsp | 1/3 cup | 2 1/2 oz | 80 ml | | 1/4 cup (1/8 Imp pt) | 2 1/2 oz |
| | | 3 1/2 oz | 100 ml | | | |
| 8 tbsp | 1/2 cup | 4 oz | 125 ml | (1/8 litre) | | |
| 10 tbsp | 2/3 cup | 5 oz | 160 ml | | 1/2 cup (1/4 Imp pt) | 5 oz |
| 12 tbsp | 3/4 cup | 6 oz | 180 ml | | | |
| | | 6 1/2 oz | 200 ml | | | |
| 16 tbsp | 1 cup | 8 oz | 250 ml | (1/4 litre) | | |
| | | 10 oz | 300 ml | | 1 cup (1/2 Imp pt) | 10 oz |
| | 1 1/2 cup | 12 oz | 375 ml | | | |
| (1 pint) | 2 cups | 16 oz | 500 ml | (1/2 litre) | | |
| | | 20 oz | 600 ml | | 2 cup (1 Imp pt) | 20 oz |
| (1 1/2 pt) | 3 cups | 24 oz | 750 ml | | | |
| (1 quart) | 4 cups | 32 oz | 1,000 ml | (1 litre) | 1 3/4 Imp pt | |
| (2 quarts) | 8 cups | 64 oz | 2,000 ml | (2 litre) | 3 1/2 Imp pt | |
| (1 gallon) | 16 cups | 128 oz | 4,000 ml | (4 litre) | | |

# Tables

| DRY INGREDIENTS | | |
|---|---|---|
| Pounds | Imperial | Metric |
| | 1/2 oz | 15 g |
| | 1 oz | 30 g |
| | 1 1/2 oz | 45 g |
| 1/8 lb | 2 oz | 60 g |
| | 2 1/2 oz | 75 g |
| | 3 oz | 85 g |
| | 3 1/2 oz | 100 g |
| 1/4 lb | 4 oz | 125 g |
| | 5 oz | 150 g |
| | 6 oz | 180 g |
| | 6 1/2 oz | 200 g |
| 1/2 lb | 8 oz | 250 g |
| | 9 oz | 280 g |
| | 9 1/2 oz | 300 g |
| 3/4 lb | 12 oz | 350 g |
| | 14 oz | 440 g |
| | 15 oz | 470 g |
| 1 lb | 16 oz | 500 g |
| 1 3/4 lb | 20 oz | 750 g |
| 2 lb | 22 oz | 1 kg |
| 3 lb | 38 oz | 1.5 kg |

| MEASUREMENTS FOR DRINKS | |
|---|---|
| 1 dash | 6 drops |
| 1/4 tsp | 15 drops |
| 1/2 tsp | 30 drops |
| 1 tsp (5 ml) | 60 drops |
| 3 tsp | 1 tbsp |
| 1 tbsp (15 ml) | 1/2 fluid oz |
| 1 pony (30 ml) | 1 fluid oz |
| 2 tbsp | 1 oz |
| 1 jigger | 1 1/2 fluid oz |
| 1 large jigger | 2 fluid oz |
| Standard whiskey glass | 2 oz |
| 1 Gill (US 1/4 pt) | 4 fluid oz |
| 1 Gill (UK 1/4 pt) | 5 fluid oz |
| 1 pint (500 ml) | 16 fluid oz |
| 1 fifth | 25.6 fluid oz |
| 1 qt (1000 ml) | 32 fluid oz |

| LENGTH | |
|---|---|
| Imperial | Metric |
| 1/4 inch | .7 cm |
| 1/2 inch | 1.3 cm |
| 3/4 inch | 2 cm |
| 1 inch | 2.5 cm |
| 2 inches | 5 cm |
| 3 inches | 7.5 cm |
| 4 inches | 10 cm |
| 6 inches | 15 cm |
| 8 inches | 20.5 cm |
| 9 inches | 23 cm |
| 10 inches | 25.5 cm |
| 12 inches | 30.5 cm |
| 18 inches | 46 cm |
| 20 inches | 51 cm |
| 24 inches | 61 cm |

| OVEN TEMPRATURE CHART | | | |
|---|---|---|---|
| Heat | ° F | ° C | Gas |
| Very Slow Oven | 250 | 120 | 1/2 |
| Slow Oven | 300 | 150 | 1-2 |
| Moderately Slow | 325 | 160 | 3 |
| Moderate Oven | 350 | 180 | 4 |
| Moderately Hot | 375 | 190 | 5-6 |
| Hot Oven | 400 | 200 | 6-7 |
| Very Hot Oven | 450 | 230 | 8-9 |
| Broil or Grill | 550 | 280 | 10 |

# Index

## A

## B

# *Acknowledgements*

RESEARCH AND CREATIVE DOCUMENTATION
Valerie Facey · Nancy Sutherland
Christine Nunes · Winnie Risden Hunter


Art Direction and Design: Valerie Facey
Layout: Quantum Design
Executive Editor: Valerie Facey


PHOTOGRAPHY
Kent Reid
Cover detail of painting *Cocoa Walks* by I.M. Belisario
Courtesy of The National Gallery of Jamaica


The Mill Press gratefully acknowledges the
assistance of the following persons:
Charlie Browne, John Pringle, Maurice Facey, Winston Stona
Jackie Ranston, Olive Senior
Tony Aarons, George Proctor, Trevor Wong
John Burrowes, Michael Lyn, Richard Scholefield
Mario Machado, Gerard Resnick, C.E.C.
Marion Burgess, Wendy Facey, Gloria Green, Dorothy Shirley
as well as
all the many friends and advisors worldwide
who have promoted and encouraged the idea of this book.

"Song of the Banana Man" (page 47)
Courtesy of Evan Jones

"Lady Nugent's Jounal, March 1802" (page 71)
Courtesy of Institute of Jamaica

Printed and bound in Jamaica by
Stephensons Litho Press Limited